Minilessons for Extending Addition and Subtraction

A Yearlong Resource

CATHERINE TWOMEY FOSNOT

WILLEM UITTENBOGAARD

DEDICATED TO TEACHERS™

*first*hand
An imprint of Heinemann
361 Hanover Street
Portsmouth, NH 03801–3912
firsthand.heinemann.com

ISBN 13: 978-0-325-01102-8
ISBN 10: 0-325-01102-8

SCHOOL PUBLISHERS

Harcourt School Publishers
6277 Sea Harbor Drive
Orlando, FL 32887–6777
www.harcourtschool.com

ISBN 13: 978-0-15-360569-7
ISBN 10: 0-15-360569-3

The development of a portion of the material described within was supported in part by the National Science Foundation under Grant No. 9911841. Any opinions, findings, and conclusions or recommendations expressed in these materials are those of the authors and do not necessarily reflect the views of the National Science Foundation.

Library of Congress Cataloging-in-Publication Data
CIP data is on file with the Library of Congress

Printed in the United States of America on acid-free paper

16 15 14 13   ML   6 7 8 9

Acknowledgements

Photography

Herbert Seignoret
Mathematics in the City, City College of New York

Schools featured in photographs

The Muscota New School/PS 314 (an empowerment school in Region 10), New York, NY
Independence School/PS 234 (Region 9), New York, NY
Fort River Elementary School, Amherst, MA

Contents

Contents *Continued*

The Money Model

Twenty Questions

Strings

Overview

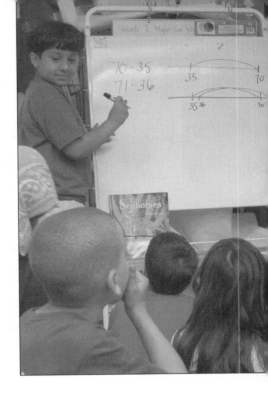

U nlike many of the other units in the *Contexts for Learning Mathematics* series, which consist of two-week sequences of investigations and related minilessons, this unit is meant to be used as a resource of 68 minilessons that you can choose from throughout the year. In contrast to investigations, which constitute the heart of the math workshop, the minilesson is more guided and more explicit, designed to be used at the start of math workshop and to last for ten to fifteen minutes. Each day, no matter what other unit or materials you are using, you might choose a minilesson from this resource to help your students develop efficient computation. You can also use them with small groups of children as you differentiate instruction.

This guide is structured progressively, moving from the use of counting and place value activities, to the use of a connecting cube train (as a number line) allowing for counting if needed but where the five- and ten-structures are emphasized, to the open number line where mental jumps of numbers being added or subtracted are recorded. The last section supports the use of coins to establish helpful landmark numbers. Although you may not use every minilesson in this resource, you will want to work through it with a developmental progression in mind.

Except for the first section, which is made up of counting and place value activities, the bulk of the minilessons in this resource unit are crafted as groups, or "strings," of tightly structured computation problems designed to encourage children to look to the numbers first, before they decide on a computation strategy. The strings are crafted to support the development of a variety of mental math strategies as well as the traditional algorithms. These strings are likely to generate discussion on certain strategies or big ideas underlying an understanding of addition and subtraction.

The Mathematical Landscape: Developing Numeracy

Try an experiment. Calculate 3996 + 4246. Don't read on until you have an answer. If you are like most people who are products of the American school system, you probably got a pencil and paper, wrote the numbers in columns, added the units and regrouped, then added each remaining column, right to left. You used the regrouping algorithm—the procedures you were taught in school. If you didn't, congratulations! You probably have number sense.

What would someone with good number sense do? What would a mathematician do? Both would look to the numbers first to decide on a strategy. Because 3996 is so close to the more friendly number 4000, a more efficient strategy would be to remove 4 from 4246 resulting in 4242. Combining the 4 with 3996 establishes an equivalent form of the problem, 4000 + 4242, which is easy to calculate mentally. But what if the numbers can't be made friendly so easily? Try 234 + 136. You could use 235 + 135, or 240 + 130: the answer is 370. Or try 289 + 79. You could use 290 + 80 − 2, or maybe 300 + 80 − 11 − 1: the answer is 368. If you try to find numbers that can't be made friendly—numbers where the algorithm (the regrouping procedure) is faster—you will probably discover that the only time the regrouping algorithm is the best strategy is when you are calculating long columns of numbers. And today when we have many large numbers to add, we use a calculator.

How about subtraction? Let's try 3400 − 189. Do you need pencil and paper? You could just add 11 to each number; the equivalent result, 3411 − 200, can be done mentally quite easily. Consider the age difference between a 71-year-old and a 36-year-old. A year ago they were 70 and 35, but the difference was the same (71 − 36 = 70 − 35). Any subtraction problem can be made friendlier just by thinking about subtraction as the difference between two numbers on a number line. Just slide the numbers back and forth, while keeping the difference constant, until you reach a nice landmark number that makes the subtraction easy.

Regrouping can be a challenge with 3400 − 189 because of the zeroes — at least it is a challenge for children, as researchers have well documented. If they attempt to regroup, they often make many place value mistakes and lose sight of the actual numbers, arriving at quite unreasonable answers. Yet, because they trust in the algorithm, they assume they are correct. Many children end up with 3389 because they take 0 away from 89. They don't stop to wonder how taking away almost 200 could result in a number almost identical to what they started with. They trust their understanding of the algorithm, rather than making an assessment of reasonableness.

To be successful in today's world, we need a deep conceptual understanding of mathematics. We are bombarded with numbers, statistics, advertisements, and similar data every day—on the Internet, on the radio, on television, and in newspapers. We need good mental ability and good number sense in order to evaluate advertising claims, estimate quantities,

efficiently calculate the numbers we deal with every day and judge whether these calculations are reasonable, add up restaurant checks and determine equal shares, interpret data and statistics, and so on. We need a deep understanding of number and operation that allows us to both estimate and make exact calculations mentally. This understanding includes algorithms, but it places emphasis on mental arithmetic and a repertoire of strategies.

Depending on the numbers, the algorithm is often slow. It only seems faster to most adults because they have always used algorithms. The procedures have become habits that require little thinking. Calculating with number sense as a mathematician means having many strategies at your disposal and looking to the numbers first *before* choosing a strategy. How do we, as teachers, develop children's ability to do this? How do we engage them in learning to be young mathematicians at work?

Using Minilessons to Develop Number Sense: An Example

Minilessons are usually done with the whole class together in a meeting area. Young children often sit on a rug; for older students, benches or chairs can be placed in a U-shape. Clustering students together like this, near a chalkboard, is helpful because you will want to provide an opportunity for pair talk at times, and you will need space to represent the strategies that will become the focus of discussion. The problems are written one at a time and learners are asked to determine an answer. Although the emphasis is on the development of mental arithmetic strategies, this does not mean learners have to solve the problems *in* their heads—but it is important for them to do the problems *with* their heads! In other words, encourage children to examine the numbers in the problem and think about clever, efficient ways to reach a solution. The relationships among the problems in the minilesson will support children in doing this. By developing a repertoire of strategies, an understanding of the big ideas underlying why they work, and a variety of ways to model the relations, children are developing powerful toolboxes for flexible and efficient computation. Enter a classroom with us and see how this is done.

"I broke the 15 into a 10 and a 4 and a 1." Brittani, a second grader in New York City, is explaining how she solved the problem 15 + 9. "Then I gave the 1 to the 9, that made 10 . . . and I knew that 10 plus 10 was 20, and 4 more made 24."

Brittani's teacher, Jennifer, has chosen the numbers in her string to encourage children to make use of 10 when they add. Ten can be helpful in several ways:

- By taking leaps of ten all at once and adjusting—for example, 15 + 9 = 15 + 10 − 1.

- By moving to the next multiple of 10—for example, 15 + 9 = 15 + 5 (to get 20, the next multiple of 10) + 4.

- By using compensation to make a problem with 10 in it—for example, 15 + 9 = 14 + 10.

Jennifer began with 15 + 10 and then moved to 15 + 9, because the number 9 is so close to 10. She anticipated that some children, noticing that, would make a leap of ten and subtract 1, effectively bringing the strategy up for discussion. The third problem in her string is 15 + 19. This addend (19) is 10 more than the 9 in the second problem. Here Jennifer anticipates that whatever strategy her students have found effective in the second problem will be extended in the third. If children simply count, without using 10, patterns will still appear in the answers that are likely to engender discussion. Her fourth problem (28 + 19) will challenge the children further. Will they use an equivalent expression: 28 + 20 − 1 or 30 + 17? The next problem (28 + 32) is similar; will they do 28 + 30 + 2 or make the problem 30 + 30? In the last problem (39 + 21), she hopes that even children who were not initially making use of the tens will do so here, after the discussion, since 39 is so close to 40, and 21 is so close to 20. She anticipates that many children now will see how easy it is to use an equivalent form, 40 + 20.

Although Jennifer had thought about the problems beforehand and had the string she is using ready, she does not put all the problems on the board at once. Instead, she writes one at a time, and children discuss their strategies before the subsequent problem is presented. This way, the children can consider the strategies from the previous problem as well as the numbers, and they are prompted to think about the relationships of the

problems in the string as they go along. Sometimes, depending on the strategies she hears, Jennifer adjusts the problems in her planned string on the spot to ensure that the strategies she is attempting to develop are discussed and tried out. For example, if none of the children use ten when they solve 15 + 9, Jennifer might insert two more problems that use ten explicitly—27 + 10, 32 + 10—and then return to the 9 with a problem like 32 + 9.

Brittani is beginning to make tens, but to do so she writes the 15 as three addends (10 + 4 + 1)—a slower, more cumbersome strategy. For just that reason, Jennifer begins the discussion with this strategy and uses it as a scaffold for more efficient strategies.

After Brittani shares her strategy, Jennifer paraphrases, drawing three short lines from the number 15 to represent the split. "So you broke up the 15 into 10, 4, and 1." She writes these numbers under the 15 as in the figure below:

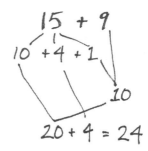

"Then you made another 10 with the 1 and the 9." She draws lines connecting these numbers. "And then you added the tens to make 20, and the 4 left made 24?"

By representing children's strategies, Jennifer provides a written record of the action. This allows other children to "see" the strategy; it becomes a picture that can be discussed. Purely verbal explanations are often too difficult for children to understand, particularly when the strategy being described is different from the one they used. Having a representation of the action allows more children to understand and to take part in the discussion.

"Any questions for Brittani? Did anybody do it a different way? Luke?"

"I used the hundred chart," says Luke, pointing to the large pocket chart containing the numbers 1 through 100, that hangs next to the chalkboard, "and I took 1 away."

Although Jennifer's goal is to *develop* mental math strategies, that does not mean that during the minilesson children must *use* mental strategies. Although Brittani has solved the computation mentally, Luke has not.

"Show us, Luke," Jennifer says.

"I started with 15, and I jumped down a row to 25. Then I took 1 away." Luke points to the numbers on the chart as he explains.

Although Jennifer knows why he took 1 away, she is aware that this is a difficult leap in thinking for many of her beginning second graders. So she asks Luke to elaborate: "Tell us why you took 1 away."

Although Luke understands why he took 1 away, he struggles to communicate his reasoning to his classmates: "Because I knew 15 plus 10 was 25, but I needed to take 1 away." Other children begin to question him.

"But why, Luke?" Katia asks, puzzled. "How did you know to take 1 away?"

This time Luke's response is clearer: "Because I only needed 9, not 10." Several children, including Katia and Brittani, now nod with understanding and agreement. Although Luke has not solved the problem mentally — he has used the hundred chart as a tool — his strategy is very efficient. He has kept the 15 whole and made use of the fact that 9 is close to 10. He takes a leap of 10 all at once and subtracts 1 at the end. Because the hundred chart is structured in tens, children often notice the patterns and begin to move vertically on it rather than only horizontally. When they move vertically, they are taking leaps of ten; when they move horizontally, they are counting by ones. Although they notice and use the patterns on the hundred chart, they are not necessarily thinking of leaps of ten mentally, however. This is an important landmark strategy — one that Jennifer wants to highlight in this minilesson.

To do so, she models Luke's strategy on the open number line:

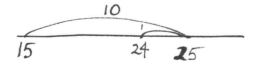

She wants Luke to think in leaps of ten, mentally, on a number line without needing the hundred chart as a manipulative. By connecting the hundred chart to the open number line, she attempts to help all the children move from a tool—a model of their thinking—to a more formal mathematical model *for* thinking—a number line.

"So you took a leap of ten," she paraphrases as she draws the leap on the number line and writes 10 above it and 25 under it. "And then you went back 1 because you only needed to add 9." Jennifer writes 1 and marks a small leap backward, completing the representation by writing 24. "Wow, that's a neat strategy, isn't it?" she finishes, inviting the class to reflect on Luke's strategy.

Although the next problem in the string that Jennifer has prepared is 15 + 19, she decides to try 15 + 8 instead. She wants to see whether children will make use of Luke's strategy. Underneath the last problem, which now reads 15 + 9 = 24, she writes 15 + 8. "Show me with thumbs-up when you have an answer." After giving an appropriate amount of think time, which she gauges by looking at the number of thumbs up, she starts a discussion. "Tyler?"

"It's 23. Because like Luke said, he jumped down 10 and went back 1. That was 24. So I jumped back 2."

Jennifer draws another open number line to represent Tyler's thinking:

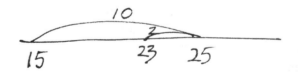

"Neat, you used Luke's idea." Luke smiles broadly. "How many of you did it that way?" Several hands go up. "Did anybody do it a different way? Karen?"

Although it seems a simple step to go from 15 + 9 = 24 to 15 + 8 = 24 − 1, and many children do see this relationship, Karen does not. She sees it as a separate problem, and she needs to make sense of it for herself.

"Can I use the string of cubes?" Karen points to the 50 connecting cubes (in groups of 5 in alternating colors) on a wire, which Jennifer has made and strung across the top of the chalkboard.

"Sure," Jennifer says. "What do you want me to push over?"

"Fifteen," Karen responds tentatively.

"OK, so here's 10." Jennifer deliberately slides over two groups of 5 in order to reinforce children's understanding, and use, of ten. "So how many more do I need?" Will Karen know immediately that 5 more are needed, or will she have to count?

"You need 5 more," Karen responds.

"OK." Jennifer moves them over. "And what do you want to add?"

"Add 8."

"OK, here's 10 more." Jennifer moves over two groups of 5, again attempting to support the development of strategies based on tens. "How can I make this into 8?"

"Take 2 off," Karen answers, and Jennifer moves 2 cubes back to the right.

"If we started with 15, how many more would we need to get 20?" Jennifer points to the cubes as she attempts to stretch Karen's thinking toward compensation.

"Five more."

"Okay," Jennifer agrees, and shifts 5 cubes over to the left, making 20 and 3. "So we know it's 23?"

Although children may initially compute problems in a string in various ways, as they share their strategies they notice and discuss patterns in the string and in the answers. They become intrigued by the fact that answers are the same, or that they are different by one or by ten, and they want to investigate why these patterns are occurring. They are impressed by, and interested in, their classmates' strategies and often adopt them when the strategies seem appropriate and more efficient. These young mathematicians are composing and decomposing numbers flexibly as they add. They are inventing their own strategies. They are looking for relationships among the problems. They are looking at the numbers first before they decide on a strategy.

Children don't do this automatically. Jennifer has worked to develop this ability in her students by focusing on computation every day, during minilessons with strings of related problems. She has developed the big ideas and models through investigations, but once this understanding has been constructed, she promotes fluency with computation strategies in minilessons such as this one.

Using Models during Minilessons

An important component of the mathematical landscape is the development of mathematical modeling. In her minilesson, Jennifer makes use of several tools, representations, and models. She uses short lines to represent splitting. She uses the open number line to represent other strategies. Children go back and forth from the hundred chart to the string of connecting cubes to the open number line. While the hundred chart is likely to encourage the use of leaps of ten, because children can make use of columns, the train of connecting cubes in alternating groups of five is more likely to support use of the five-structure. But because the hundred chart and the cubes allow children to count by ones, their use can lead to a reading-off approach, rather than promoting the ability to calculate mentally. In contrast, the open number line encourages children to think about landmarks on a number line, to take the leaps mentally, and to visualize the landing points, rather than to simply read off the answer. Another limitation of the hundred chart is that it is not a linear representation of numbers as on a number line, but instead is analogous to prose, as read on a page. After 10 comes 11, but one must shift to the left and go down a line to find it. This can be a problem for children when they are developing a "number space"—a model to think with.

As you do minilessons from this resource unit, you will want to use models to depict children's strategies. Representing computation strategies with mathematical models provides children with images for discussion, and supports the development of the various strategies for computational fluency. The connecting cube train, the open number line, and money are the primary models used in this guide for addition and subtraction—assuming that the models have already been developed with realistic situations and rich investigations. In the *Contexts for Learning Mathematics* series, the units *Measuring for the Art Show* and *Ages and Timelines* can be used to develop the connecting cube and open number line models. The money model is developed in the *Contexts for Learning Mathematics* unit *The T-Shirt Factory*. If your students do not clearly understand the use of these models, you may find it beneficial to use the relevant units first. Once the model has been introduced as a representation of a realistic situation, you can use it to model the computation strategies that children explain.

A Few Words of Caution

As you work with the minilessons in this resource book, it is very important to remember two things. First, honor children's strategies. Accept alternative solutions and explore why they work. Use the models to represent children's strategies and facilitate discussion and reflection on the strategies shared. Sample classroom episodes (titled "Inside One Classroom") are interspersed throughout this resource guide to help you anticipate what learners might say and do, and to provide you with images of teachers and children at work. The intent is not to get all learners to use the same strategy at the end of the string. That would simply be discovery learning. The strings are crafted to support development, to encourage children to look to the numbers and to use a variety of strategies helpful for those numbers.

Second, do not use the string as a recipe that cannot be varied. You will need to be flexible. The strings are designed to encourage discussion and reflection on various strategies important for numeracy. Although the strings have been carefully crafted to support the development of these strategies, they are not foolproof: if the numbers in the string are not sufficient to produce the results intended, you will need to insert additional problems, depending on your students' responses, to provide more opportunities for learning. For this reason, most of the strings are accompanied by a Behind the Numbers section describing the string's purpose and how the numbers were chosen. Being aware of the purpose of each string will guide you in determining what type of problems to add. These sections should also be helpful in developing your ability to craft your own strings. Strings are fun both to do and to craft.

Resources

Dolk, Maarten, and Catherine Twomey Fosnot. 2004a. *Addition and Subtraction Minilessons, Grades PreK–3.* CD-ROM with accompanying facilitator's guide by Antonia Cameron, Sherrin B. Hersch, and Catherine Twomey Fosnot. Portsmouth, NH: Heinemann.

———. 2004b. *Fostering Children's Mathematical Development, Grades PreK–3: The Landscape of Learning.* CD-ROM with accompanying facilitator's guide by Sherrin B. Hersch, Antonia Cameron and Catherine Twomey Fosnot. Portsmouth, NH: Heinemann.

Around the Circle

Counting around the circle can be a very helpful activity for exploring number patterns. In this guide, it is used to explore addition and subtraction of tens, hundreds, and thousands. Place value, equivalence, and the addition and subtraction of landmarks and near landmarks are the focus of this first section.

Adding Tens, Place Value

Have children sit in a circle in the meeting area. Ask one child to choose a number between 1 and 9. Write it at the top of a large sheet of chart paper. Go around the circle having each child add 10 to the previous number. Record the results on the chart. For example, if a child chooses 3, you would be recording 13, 23, 33, 43, 53, etc. Discuss the pattern: the number of tens increases by one each time, while the number of units stays the same. Ask: Will this always happen? Try a few more numbers. For example, start with 7 or 8, adding 10 repeatedly, as before. Ask children why they think the pattern is occurring.

Behind the Numbers

This minilesson was designed to support the development of an understanding of place value. Discuss how the pattern continues past 100 — for example, 93, 103, 113, and 123. Help the children notice that the pattern is continuing — the number of tens increases by one each time, while the number of units stays the same. Do *not* focus on the columns or ask: How many hundreds, how many tens? Thinking of 113 only as 1 hundred, 1 ten, and 3 units obscures the increasing tens pattern. Establish that 1 hundred has 10 tens, so 1 hundred plus 1 ten makes 11 tens. Develop the idea of equivalence: that 113 can be thought of as 11 tens and 3 units, and also as 1 hundred, 1 ten, and 3 units.

A Portion of the Minilesson

Inside One Classroom

Joan (the teacher): So let's see what we have so far: 3, 13, 23, 33, 43, and it's your turn Natasha....what comes next?

Natasha: *(Counting on her fingers by ones.)* Fifty-three. *(Joan adds 53 to the list.)*

Ricardo: Hey! There's a pattern.

Joan: What are you noticing? Tell us more.

Ricardo: It's going 1, 2, 3, 4, 5, like that. It's going up.

Erika: Yeah. And the other number is staying the same. It's always 3.

Author's Notes

After several numbers are listed Joan repeats the list. Sometimes just hearing the list aloud can help children begin to notice patterns.

Joan does not explain the pattern. She invites the young mathematicians to examine it. Noticing patterns and determining why they are occurring is an important aspect of mathematics.

continued on next page

continued from previous page

Joan: That's interesting, isn't it? Hmmm. Let's see if it keeps happening. *(Several more numbers are added, 63, 73, 83, 93, 103.)*

Natasha: It's not happening. Now it's 0.

Ricardo: No it still is…it went from 9 to 10.

Joan: What will the next one be?

Natasha: Oh yeah…113. Now it is 11.

Joan: So what's going on here? What is this 11? Turn to the person next to you and discuss this for a few minutes. *(After several minutes of pair talk, the whole group conversation resumes.)* Sue…what did you and Rodney talk about?

Sue: We think it's because we are adding a ten…so the tens are going up.

Natasha: But the tens aren't always going up. See… it's 9, then 0 *(referring to 93 and 103)*.

Ricardo: Yeah, but the number of tens is going up. Before there were 9 tens, then 10 tens.

Joan: How many groups of ten are there in 103?

Ricardo: Ten tens in 100…so 10, and 3 left over.

Joan: So we could think about 103 as 1 hundred, 0 tens, 3 ones. I think that is how you are seeing it Natasha? Or as 10 tens and 3 ones like Ricardo is seeing it. Are they both right? Talk to the person next you about this.

Pair talk is used as a way to focus everyone on the issue at hand.

Children are encouraged to make sense of place value for themselves.

Pair talk is used again to focus on equivalence.

Around the Circle · A2

Adding Nine by Adding Ten and Subtracting One, Place Value, Equivalence

This minilesson is similar to A1, but 9 is added instead of 10. Adding 9 is equivalent to adding $10 - 1$. As with A1, focus on the total number of tens, not the digit in the tens place. See page 12 for further information.

Behind the Numbers

This minilesson was designed to support the development of an understanding of place value, equivalence, and particularly the strategy of adding 9 by adding 10 and then subtracting 1.

Adding Twenty, Place Value

This minilesson is similar to A1, but 20 is added instead of 10. Go around the circle having each child add 20 to the previous number. Record the results on the chart. For example, if a child chooses 3, you would be recording 23, 43, 63, 83, 103, etc. Discuss the pattern: the number of tens increases by 2 each time and is always an even number, while the number of units stays the same. For variation, start with a number between 10 and 20 and explore why the resulting number of tens is now odd. What if 30 were added each time?

Behind the Numbers

This minilesson was designed to support the development of an understanding of place value. Discuss how the pattern continues past 100, for example: 83, 103, and 123. Help the children notice that the pattern is continuing: the number of tens increases by 2 each time, while the number of units stays the same. Do *not* focus on the columns and ask: How many hundreds, how many tens? Thinking of 103 as 1 hundred, 0 tens, and 3 units obscures the increasing tens pattern. Establish that 1 hundred has 10 tens, so 1 hundred plus 0 tens makes 10 tens. Focus on equivalence: 123 can be thought of as 12 tens and 3 units, and also as 1 hundred, 2 tens, and 3 units.

Subtracting Ten, Place Value

This minilesson focuses on subtracting groups of ten. Have one child choose a number between 190 and 200 and go around the circle having each child subtract 10 from the previous number. Depending on how many children you have in your class, you may not be able to go completely around the circle, but that is OK. Record the results on chart paper. For example, if a child chooses 193, you would be recording 183, 173, 163, 153, 143, etc. Discuss the pattern. This time the number of tens decreases by 1 each time. Ask: Will this always happen? Try a few more numbers. For example, start with 197 or 198, or ask a child to choose a number between 200 and 300, and go around the circle subtracting 10 repeatedly, as before. Ask children why they think the pattern is occurring.

Around the Circle · A5

Subtracting Nine by Subtracting Ten and Adding One, Place Value, Equivalence

Have children sit in a circle in the meeting area. Have one child choose a number between 190 and 200. Write it at the top of a large sheet of chart paper. Go around the circle having each child subtract 9 from the previous number. Do not go past 0. Most children will probably need to count backward at first. Record the results on the chart. For example, if a child chooses 193, you would be recording 184, 175, 166, 157, 148, etc. If the number of children in your class does not allow you to go all around the circle, that is OK. Discuss the pattern and explore equivalence: $-9 = -10 + 1$. For variation, have children subtract 8, or 7. Push for generalization: If the children begin by subtracting 10, do they know how much to add back in?

Around the Circle · A6

Subtracting Twenty, Place Value

This string is a variation on A5. Go around the circle having each child subtract 20 from the previous number. Record the results on chart paper. Discuss the pattern: the number of tens decreases by 2 each time and is an odd number, while the number of units stays the same. Ask: Will this always happen? Try a few more numbers. For example, start with 197 or 198, subtracting 20 repeatedly, as before. Ask children why they think the pattern is occurring. For variation, start with an even number of tens, for example 186, and explore why the resulting number of tens is now even. What if 30 were subtracted each time?

Around the Circle · A7

Adding One Hundred, Place Value

This minilesson is similar to others in this section but the focus now extends to adding a three-digit number, each time. Have one child choose a number between 10 and 100. Write it at the top of a large sheet of chart paper. Go around the circle having each child add 100 to the previous number. Record the results on the chart. For example, if a child chooses 34, you would be recording 134, 234, 334, 434, 534, etc. Discuss the pattern: the number of hundreds increases by 1 each time and the numbers of tens and units stay the same. Ask: Will this always happen? Try a few more starting numbers. You might also have children add 200 each time and note the patterns. What if you asked a child to choose a starting number between 100 and 200?

This minilesson was designed to support the development of an understanding of place value. Discuss how the pattern continues past 1000, for example: 934, 1034, 1134, etc. Help the children notice that the pattern is continuing: the number of hundreds increases by 1 each time. Do *not* focus on the columns and ask: How many thousands, hundreds, tens? Thinking of 1134 as 1 thousand, 1 hundred, 3 tens, and 4 units obscures the increasing hundreds pattern. Establish that 1 thousand has 10 hundreds, so 1 thousand plus 1 hundred makes 11 hundreds. Develop the idea of equivalence: that 1134 can be thought of as 11 hundreds plus 34, as well as 1 thousand, 1 hundred, 3 tens, and 4 units or as 113 tens and 4 units. For further support several more related minilessons follow.

Around the Circle · A8

Subtracting One Hundred, Place Value

Have one child choose a number between 1000 and 2000. Write it at the top of a large sheet of chart paper. Go around the circle having each child subtract 100 from the previous number. Record the results on the chart. For example, if a child chooses 1973, you would be recording 1873, 1773, 1673, etc. Discuss the pattern: the number of hundreds decreases by 1 each time and the numbers of tens and units stay the same. Ask: Will this always happen? Have the class try a few more starting numbers. You might also ask children to subtract 200 each time and note the patterns. What if a child chose a starting number between 100 and 200?

Around the Circle · A9

Adding Near Hundreds, Place Value, Equivalence

Have one child choose a number between 10 and 100. Write it at the top of a large sheet of chart paper. Go around the circle having each child add 101 to the previous number. Record the results on the chart. For example, if a child chooses 34, you would be recording 34, 135, 236, 337, etc. Discuss the pattern: the number of hundreds increases by 1 each time and the number of units increases by 1. Ask: Will this always happen? Have children try a few more starting numbers. You might also have children add 99 and note the patterns that result.

Around the Circle · A10

Subtracting Near Hundreds, Place Value, Equivalence

Have one child choose a number between 1000 and 2000. Write it at the top of a large sheet of chart paper. Go around the circle having each child subtract 101 from the previous number. Record the results on the chart. For example, if a child chooses 1734, you would be recording 1734, 1633, 1532, etc. Discuss the pattern: the number of hundreds decreases by 1 each time and the number of units decreases by 1 unit. Ask: Will this always happen? Have children try a few more starting numbers. You might also have children subtract 99 and note the patterns.

Behind the Numbers

Establish that 1 thousand has 10 hundreds, so 1 thousand plus 1 hundred makes 11 hundreds. Develop the idea of equivalence: that 1134 can be thought of as 11 hundreds plus 34, as well as 1 thousand, 1 hundred, 3 tens, and 4 units. Thus, subtracting 101 (a hundred and a one) makes the result 1033. Subtracting 99 is equivalent to subtracting 100 and then adding 1.

Around the Circle · A11

Adding and Subtracting Greater Numbers, Place Value

Have one child choose a number between 10 and 20. Write it at the top of a large sheet of chart paper. Go around the circle having each child add 1000 to the previous number, or for variation you could have each child add 1,000,000. Record the results on the chart. For example, if a child chooses 17, you would be recording 17, 1017, 2017, etc. (or, if adding 1,000,000, then 17, 1,000,017, 2,000,017, etc.) Discuss the pattern. Ask: Will this always happen? Have the class try a few more starting numbers. You might also ask children to subtract 1000 or 1,000,000 and note the patterns. Explore with the children how large the starting number needs to be if the class is to go around the circle subtracting 1,000,000.

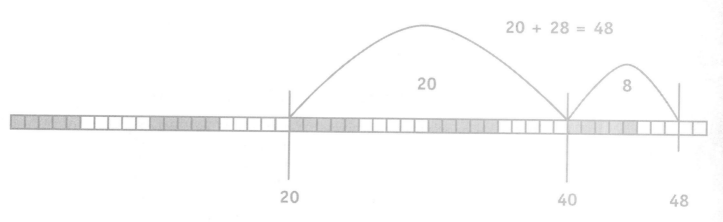

$20 + 28 = 48$

20   8

20   40   48

The Open Number Line with Connecting Cubes

In contrast to a number line with counting numbers written below, an open number line is just an empty line used to record children's addition and subtraction strategies. Only the numbers children use are recorded, and the operations are recorded as leaps, or jumps. Representations on a number line can help children move beyond tedious strategies such as counting by ones to more efficient strategies such as taking leaps of ten, decomposing numbers, and using landmark numbers. Initially, a train of cubes of two colors in alternating groups of five cubes of each color is used as a bridge to support children who may still need to count by ones. The train of cubes allows for counting by ones if needed. By using groups of five in alternating colors, the five-structure is also provided as a support and thus it provides a bridge to the open number line where only the numbers used in children's strategies are recorded. This section (B1 – B15) makes use of the connecting cubes. The following section (C1 – C32) uses only the open number line.

String · B1

Addition, Keeping One Number Whole and Taking Leaps of Ten

This string of related problems encourages children to keep one number whole and take leaps of ten. Use a train of 100 connecting cubes of two colors in alternating groups of five cubes of each color, stretched across the chalkboard (or whiteboard). Do one problem at a time. Record children's strategies by drawing the leaps as lengths on the chalkboard and use the cubes to check if needed, inviting children to comment on the representations. See Inside One Classroom, page 19. If you notice children beginning to make use of the tens, invite a discussion on why this strategy is helpful. If the class comes to a consensus that it is a useful strategy when adding, you might want to make a sign about this and post it above the meeting area.

$$26 + 10$$
$$26 + 12$$
$$26 + 22$$
$$44 + 30$$
$$44 + 39$$
$$58 + 21$$
$$63 + 29$$

Behind the Numbers: How the String was Crafted

The first problem is the scaffold for the second. Assuming that children know the pattern of adding 10, this string encourages them to use it by starting the string with it. The second expression has a value just 2 greater than the first, and the leap can be added to the number line representation of the first problem. The third expression has a value 10 greater than the second and once again the initial representation can be used — but only if children offer this strategy. The next two problems are paired, since 39 is 9 more than 30. This problem also opens the door to thinking of 39 as $40 - 1$. The last two problems support children in exploring both strategies: using the tens first and then adding the units, and taking a larger leap and subtracting at the end.

Julie (the teacher): Here's our first warm-up problem: 26 + 10. Thumbs-up when you have an answer. Michael?

Michael: It's 36. I just know.

Julie: (*Draws the following representation of Michael's strategy:*)

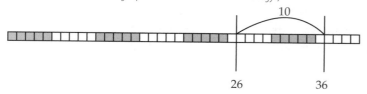

Author's Notes

Julie places the train of cubes with magnets against the chalkboard and records Michael's strategy as a leap of ten.

Does everyone agree with Michael? (*No disagreement is apparent.*) OK. Let's go to the next one: 26 + 12. Emmy?

Emmy: I added a jump of 2 more onto the last problem.

Julie: Let's see what that looks like on the number line. (*Records the jumps in a different color on Michael's number line.*)

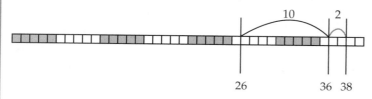

Since Emmy added two, Julie uses the same representation and just adds a jump of two.

Julie encourages the children to examine the efficiency of the strategy.

What do you think? Does Emmy's way work? Saves a lot of counting, doesn't it, if we think of 12 as 10 and 2? OK, let's go on to the next problem, 26 + 22. Show me with thumbs-up when you're ready. Susie.

Susie: It's 48, I think. I did 20 + 20 + 8.

Julie: Nice. You used the friendly number of 20 and added them. Let me record your strategy.

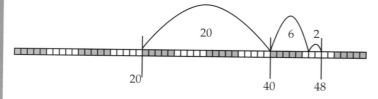

Did anybody do it a different way? Did anyone do what Emmy did last time and use the problem before?

Michael: I did. I just added on 10 more. So 38, then 48.

continued on next page

continued from previous page

Julie: Nice. It is really helpful to keep one number whole, isn't it? And just add on. Here's the next one: 44 + 30. Remember how we did all the patterns when we counted around the circle? See if that idea would be helpful here.

Abbie: It is! It's just 54, 64, 74.

Julie: How many of you agree with Abbie? Let's think about this as we continue with our string. If we agree at the end, we can make a sign and post it on our "Helpful Strategies" wall.

Alternative strategies are solicited but emphasis is placed on keeping one number whole and adding on in leaps of ten.

String · B2

Addition, Keeping One Number Whole and Taking Leaps of Ten

Like B1, this string encourages children to keep one number whole and take leaps of tens. Do one problem at a time; and record children's strategies by drawing the leaps on the chalkboard and use the cubes to check if needed, inviting other children to comment on the representations. See page 19 for further details.

$$43 + 20$$
$$43 + 24$$
$$43 + 44$$
$$52 + 30$$
$$52 + 39$$
$$68 + 22$$
$$68 + 29$$

Behind the Numbers: How the String was Crafted

The first problem is the scaffold for the second. Assuming children know the pattern of adding 10, the string encourages them to use it by starting the string with adding 2 tens. The value of the expression in the second problem is just 4 greater than the value of the first, and the leap can be added to the number line representation of the first problem. The third expression has a value 20 greater than the second and once again the initial representation can be used. The next two problems are paired, since 39 is just 9 more than 30. This problem also opens the door to thinking of 39 as 40 − 1. The last two problems support children in exploring both strategies: using the tens first and then adding the units, and taking a larger leap and subtracting at the end. For additional support, see the related strings that follow—B3 through B5.

String · B3

Addition, Keeping One Number Whole and Taking Leaps of Ten

See B2 for details (page 21).

$$36 + 30$$
$$36 + 33$$
$$36 + 36$$
$$63 + 20$$
$$63 + 29$$
$$48 + 41$$
$$48 + 29$$

Behind the Numbers: How the String was Crafted

The first problem is the scaffold for the second. Assuming children know the pattern of adding ten, this string encourages them to use it by starting the string with an addend made up of 3 tens. The sum of the second problem is just 3 more and the leap can be added to the number line representation of the first problem. The sum of the third problem is just an additional 3 more and once again the initial representation can be used. The next two problems are paired: 29 is just 9 more than 20. This problem also opens the door to thinking of 29 as $30 - 1$. The last two problems support children in exploring both strategies: using the tens first and then adding the units, and taking a larger leap and subtracting at the end.

String · B4

Addition, Keeping One Number Whole and Taking Leaps of Ten

See B2 for details (page 21).

$$53 + 30$$
$$53 + 36$$
$$53 + 46$$
$$37 + 30$$
$$37 + 39$$
$$68 + 22$$
$$68 + 29$$

String · B5

See B2 for details (page 21).

Addition, Keeping One Number Whole and Taking Leaps of Ten

75 + 20

75 + 25

75 + 24

55 + 30

55 + 39

69 + 21

69 + 29

String · B6

Subtraction, Keeping One Number Whole and Taking Leaps of Ten Back

Subtraction can also be represented on the train of cubes. This string encourages the splitting of the subtrahend with removal of chunks of ten first.

36 − 10

36 − 20

36 − 24

43 − 30

43 − 39

57 − 21

65 − 39

Behind the Numbers: How the String was Crafted

The first problem is the scaffold for the second. This requires taking a leap of ten back on the number line. The second problem removes another ten and the leap can be drawn onto the number line representation of the first problem. The third problem includes a removal of 4 more, and once again the initial representation can be used. The next two problems are paired: 39 is just 9 more than 30. This problem also opens the door to thinking of − 39 as − 40 + 1. The last two problems support children in exploring both strategies: removing the tens first and then a unit, and taking a larger leap and adding back at the end. For additional support see B7.

String · B7

Subtraction, Keeping One Number Whole and Taking Leaps of Ten Back

See B6 for details (page 23).

$$63 - 10$$
$$63 - 20$$
$$63 - 22$$
$$58 - 30$$
$$58 - 39$$
$$46 - 21$$
$$67 - 19$$

String · B8

Mixed Addition and Subtraction, Keeping One Number Whole and Taking Leaps of Ten

This string mixes the operations but encourages the same strategy as the previous strings — jumps of ten.

$$34 + 20$$
$$34 - 20$$
$$56 + 20$$
$$56 + 21$$
$$56 - 20$$
$$56 - 21$$
$$63 + 31$$
$$63 - 31$$

Behind the Numbers: How the String was Crafted

The first three problems constitute the scaffold for the fourth. The fourth expression has a value of just 1 greater than the third, and the leap can be drawn onto the representation of the first problem. The next two problems are paired to encourage children to remove the tens first. The last two problems have no helper problems, so children need to make their own.

String · B9

Mixed Addition and Subtraction, Removing or Adding Tens and Adjusting

This string of related problems encourages children to keep one number whole and take leaps of ten. But in contrast to the previous strings, it challenges children to use an equivalent expression—to over jump and then adjust. For example to add 19, use $+20 -1$.

$$47 + 40$$
$$47 + 39$$
$$47 - 30$$
$$47 - 29$$
$$62 - 39$$
$$43 - 29$$
$$52 - 19$$

Behind the Numbers: How the String was Crafted

The first four problems constitute two pairs—the first of each is the scaffold for the second. The last three problems invite children to use the strategy of taking leaps of ten and adjusting. No helper problems are provided so, children will need to make their own helper problems ($-20 + 1$). For additional support, see the related strings that follow—B10 and B11.

String · B10

Mixed Addition and Subtraction, Removing or Adding Tens and Adjusting

See B9 for details (above).

$$54 + 30$$
$$54 - 30$$
$$54 + 40$$
$$54 - 40$$
$$54 + 39$$
$$54 - 39$$
$$54 + 19$$
$$54 - 21$$

Behind the Numbers: How the String was Crafted

The first four problems constitute two pairs, which can serve as scaffolds for the fifth and sixth problems. The last two problems challenge children to examine whether to add or subtract first, and then adjust as needed.

Mixed Addition and Subtraction, Removing or Adding Tens and Adjusting

See B9 for details (page 25).

$$72 + 20$$
$$72 - 21$$
$$72 - 20$$
$$72 - 21$$
$$72 + 19$$
$$72 - 19$$
$$72 - 60$$
$$72 - 69$$

True or Not True? · B12

Treating Expressions as Objects and Separating Out Equivalent Quantities, Equivalence, Commutative and Associative Properties

This mental math minilesson uses the format of a string of several statements. Children decide if the statements are true or not true. The question mark is placed over the equal sign when the problem is initially written. Ask the children: is this statement true or not true? Once the community has analyzed the statement, the question mark is erased and the appropriate sign (either the equal or not-equal sign) is indicated to make it a true statement. As children share their thinking, represent one side of the statement above the connecting cube number line and the other below it. Group the numbers to match the children's strategies. For example, in analyzing $5 + 4 + 10 = 10 + 5 + 5$, some children may just compare the $5 + 5$ to $5 + 4$. This comparison can be represented in several ways. If a child says, "I knew the tens were the same, and 5 plus 4 is 1 less than 5 plus 5," you can draw the following:

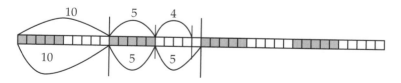

The commutative and associative properties of addition underlie this strategy. Encourage the children to discuss whether or not the order or grouping matters. As you progress through the string, encourage children to look for efficient ways of deciding whether the statement is true. Represent their strategies on the double number line to allow the community to look for equivalence, and then write the appropriate sign (= or ≠) for each problem.

$$5 + 4 + 10 \overset{?}{=} 10 + 5 + 5$$

$$13 + 4 + 7 - 4 \overset{?}{=} 3 + 13 + 4$$

$$13 + 9 + 6 \overset{?}{=} 5 + 10 + 13$$

$$6 + 3 + 10 \overset{?}{=} 8 + 3 + 7 + 2$$

Behind the Numbers: How the String was Crafted

The numbers in the string have been chosen carefully to support children in examining expressions as objects (rather than proceeding left to right with arithmetic) to determine whether the statements are true. The numbers in the first problem are almost the same on both sides. The only difference is the 4 on the left as compared with the 5 on the right. No arithmetic should be necessary to determine that the first statement is not true (the sign should be ≠), but several strategies may be used, and you may find that some of your students still need to do the arithmetic to evaluate the truth of the statement. The commutative property will probably come up for discussion because of the placement of the tens. The second problem introduces the idea of $4 - 4$, thus encouraging children to simplify the expressions by using the commutative and associative properties. The third problem has 2 thirteens, which can be subtracted from each side, but more thought will be needed for dealing with $9 + 6 = 5 + 10$. You will probably hear comments such as, "You just gain one and lose one, so the total stays the same" (compensation). This is an important idea in the development of an understanding of equivalence. The last problem may encourage children to use the associative property if they know combinations of numbers that add up to 10. The statement is not true; the sign should be ≠.

Author's Notes

Trish (the teacher): Let's try to make this problem as simple as we can, as mathematicians do. Let's look for nice, efficient ways to decide whether this is equal or not equal. *(Writes:)*

$$13 + 4 + 7 - 4 \overset{?}{=} 3 + 13 + 4$$

Efficiency and elegance of solution are valued in this community. Trish challenges the children to consider the expressions as objects instead of just doing arithmetic.

Chiara: Well, I knew 13 + 7 is 20. Then I saw 4 and minus 4, so that side is 20. It has a 4 and if you take it away... Then the other side is 13 + 7 because 3 + 4 is 7. *(Trish draws jumps of 13 + 7 above the connecting cube number line and 13 + 3 + 4 below it.)*

Trish draws the jumps above and below the connecting cube number line to provide a representation for a discussion of equivalence.

Aidan: They both have 13 and on one side there's a 7 and on the other side there's a 3 + 4.

Juanita: 3 + 4 = 7, so they each have the same on both sides.

Some of the children are beginning to eliminate equal quantities from each side and simplify the equation.

Delia: You don't have to bother with 4 − 4, because you're taking away what you just added.

Alec: I wouldn't bother looking at the 13 or the 4, because they are on both sides. And 7 take away 4 is 3, so 3 = 3.

Trish: What would 4 − 4 look like on this number line?

Delia: It would look like 4 forward [to the right] and 4 back [to the left], or chalk dust because it's nothing. *(Trish adds a jump of 4 to the previously drawn jumps and then goes back 4.)*

"Doing" and "undoing" with integers is important to algebraic thinking. The number line is used to examine the jumps.

Chynna: You don't even need to do that. It's 13 and 13, so cross them out. Cross out the 2 fours, so it's just 7 − 4 = 3.

True or Not True? · B13

Treating Expressions as Objects and Separating Out Equivalent Quantities, Equivalence, Commutative and Associative Properties

Children often work with equations very procedurally, calculating from left to right. As with B12, this string encourages them to look for more efficient ways to group and, when helpful, to separate out equivalent expressions from each side of the equal sign. Do one problem at a time; record children's strategies on the double open number line (or train of connecting cubes of two colors in alternating groups of five), inviting children to comment on the representations. If children begin to use equivalent expressions as objects, discuss why this strategy is helpful. If the class agrees that it is a useful strategy, you might want to make a sign about this and post it on a strategy wall. Use children's own words to name the strategy.

$$\overset{?}{5 + 5 = 10}$$

$$\overset{?}{2 + 5 + 5 = 10 + 2}$$

$$\overset{?}{2 + 5 + 5 = 9 + 1 + 2}$$

$$\overset{?}{2 + 8 + 5 + 5 = 2 + 10 + 8}$$

$$\overset{?}{3 + 10 + 5 = 15 + 3}$$

$$\overset{?}{3 + 15 = 10 + 5}$$

Behind the Numbers: How the String was Crafted

Since the string is designed to encourage children to use equivalent expressions, fives and tens are employed as these are friendly facts for children. This string is one of a series of strings designed to develop children's ability to treat expressions as objects. The first problem provides the scaffold. The second problem adds the same number, 2, to both sides of the equation to encourage children to use what they know, rather than performing the arithmetic procedurally left to right. The third problem requires children to set up two equivalent expressions: $5 + 5 = 9 + 1$. The fourth problem is more difficult. Now several expressions must be used in order to envision two tens on both sides. The last problem, in which the quantities on each side of the equal sign are actually unequal, is placed here to encourage children to think about how to make both sides equal.

Inside One Classroom

A Portion of the Minilesson

Trish (the teacher): So let's warm up with a string. Here's the first one, 5 + 5 = 10. True or not true? Show me with thumbs-up when you are ready. *(Most thumbs go up right away.)* Wow. You always like the way I start the strings, don't you? So I guess that was an easy one! Casey?

Casey: Equal. I just knew it!

Author's Notes

Strings begin with easy problems that can be used as a scaffold.

continued on next page

continued from previous page

Trish: Let me represent this on the open number line and then we'll go on to the next one.

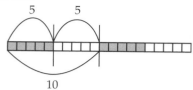

OK, here it is: 2 + 5 + 5 = 10 + 2. True or not true? Nell?

Although this is a fact nearly all the children know, Trish represents the equivalence on the double open number line. This representation can be used later in the string if children begin to use 5 + 5.

Nell: True. I did 5 + 2, that was 7, then 5 more. That's…12. The other side is 12, too.

Nell does what most children do at first when asked to examine equations: she does arithmetic.

Trish: *(Draws Nell's strategy:)*

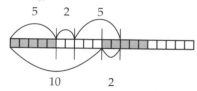

Who agrees with Nell, that this is a true statement? *(All hands go up.)* OK. Did anyone have a different way to prove it? Debbie?

Trish accepts and records all strategies so the community can examine them. Alternative strategies are valued. Although Nell's strategy is not what Trish is trying to encourage, it is Nell's conception at the start of work on this concept (shared by many others in the class).

Debbie: I used the first problem, because 5 + 5 is 10, so those are the same, and 2 is on both sides.

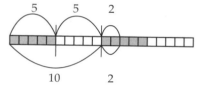

Trish: *(Recording the strategy as above.)* So do you mean you didn't even do any calculating? You just knew the amounts would be the same?

Debbie: Yep…because both sides have 10 and 2.

Trish: What do you think, Nell?

Trish brings Nell back into the conversation to encourage her to examine a more efficient strategy than the one she used.

Nell: Her way works, too. It's sort of like the symmetry we did for our art project.

Trish: Tell us more. How is it the same?

Nell: It's like the same on the top as on the bottom.

Trish: And if it is the same, then do we know it is a true statement? *(Children nod.)* What about if it is not the same, but it is equivalent…like 5 + 5…and 10?

Nell: Yes, that's OK, too. You really don't have to do the arithmetic. Debbie's way is easier.

Most children have no trouble understanding that 10 + 3 = 10 + 3, or even that 3 + 10 = 10 + 3 (commutative), but understanding that 5 + 5 is equivalent to 10 and that one equivalent expression can be substituted for another is quite another story. Here Trish challenges the class with that idea.

Treating Expressions as Objects and Separating Out Equivalent Quantities, Equivalence, Commutative and Associative Properties

See B13 for details (page 28).

$$25 + 4 \stackrel{?}{=} 4 + 10 + 10 + 5$$

$$25 + 6 + 4 - 6 \stackrel{?}{=} 4 + 10 + 10 + 5$$

$$10 + 10 + 5 + 13 \stackrel{?}{=} 13 + 28 + 25 - 28$$

$$10 + 15 + 13 \stackrel{?}{=} 18 + 10 + 10$$

Behind the Numbers: How the String was Crafted

The numbers have been chosen carefully to support children in making equivalent expressions, a strategy that can be used to determine whether the statements are true. The problems have been crafted to encourage a conversation about the commutative and associative properties for addition. The first equation uses the landmark numbers of 5, 10, and 25 to encourage children to group (10, 10, and 5 into 25). The connecting cube train can be used to explore why it is OK to do this (because of the associative property). In the next step, children are faced with proving that $25 + 4 = 4 + 25$, which is possible because of the commutative property. The representation supports children in generalizing these properties.

The second problem adds the expression $6 - 6$ to the previous problem in order to suggest the importance of grouping. Help children realize that although these numbers are not next to each other in the problem, they still sum to zero, so now the equation is identical to the first. The third problem uses the same idea, but employs greater numbers ($28 - 28$) to make the arithmetic more challenging. If some children are still performing tedious arithmetic operations from left to right, these numbers serve to discourage that strategy. The last problem is a little more difficult because it requires children to decompose numbers in order to make their own equivalent expressions.

Treating Expressions as Objects and Separating Out Equivalent Quantities, Equivalence, Commutative and Associative Properties

Children decide if each statement in this string is true or not true; if a statement is not true, children must use the not-equal sign to make it true as they did in the previous strings. With this string however, a variable is introduced as a secret number that you are adding to both sides of the equation. Be sure the children understand that it is the same number on both sides. Ask them to think about what the number might be. As they generate several possibilities, try them out (re-writing the equation with the suggested number), to help the class realize that the statement is true for any number, even for zero. In the last problem, challenge children to analyze what happens when N = 0.

$$5 + 20 + 4 \overset{?}{=} 4 + 10 + 15$$

$$N + 5 + 20 + 4 \overset{?}{=} 4 + 10 + 15 + N$$

$$13 + 8 + 6 \overset{?}{=} 5 + 9 + 13$$

$$13 + 8 \overset{?}{=} 5 + 9 + 13 - 6$$

$$8 + 6 \overset{?}{=} 5 + 9 + N$$

Behind the Numbers: How the String was Crafted

The numbers have been chosen carefully to support children in considering expressions as objects, using the commutative and associative properties, subtracting equal quantities from each side of an equation, and realizing that adding the same number to each side of an equation maintains equivalence. The first two equations are identical except for the addition of N to the second. The third and fourth equations are also related. Adding 6 to each side of the fourth equation results in the third equation. Children usually see the last equation, at first, as having unequal amounts on each side of the equal sign, since N is only on one side. If they fail to consider what happens if N = 0, ask them to do so, and help them realize that the statement is true if and only if N = 0.

A Portion of the Minilesson

Inside One Classroom

Trish (the teacher)**:** How about this next one:

$13 + 8 \overset{?}{=} 5 + 9 + 13 - 6$. True or not true?

Ian: Equal. Because 13 is on both sides so I can cancel those out. And $5 + 9$ is 14 and $14 - 6$ is 8. And 8 equals 8.

Chynna: My way is different. I started with the 9 and took 6 away. That left me with $13 + 8 = 8 + 13$. And I know that is equal because the numbers can be turned around.

Trish: I'll share my way, but I don't know if it will work all the time. Tell me what you think. I used the problem before this one: $13 + 8 + 6 = 5 + 9 + 13$. I took 6 away from both sides, and since I knew the first problem was true I thought this one had to be, too. What do you think?

Rosie: That works! All the time…because if you add or subtract any number to both sides and it's the same number it will stay the same.

Trish: So what about this one? True or not true? I'll use N to mean a secret number again. *(Writes:)* $8 + 6 = 5 + 9 + N$.

Chiara: Not equal because if you add a number on only one side it won't work.

Trish: Talk to the person next to you about what Chiara said. Do you agree? *(After a few moments of pair talk.)* Roxanna, what did your partner and you decide?

Roxanna: Mostly we agree, but what if the secret number is zero? Then it's true.

Trish: So this is true only when N equals zero?

Author's Notes

Several children share their strategies for establishing equivalence.

Trish shares her strategy. Removing six from both sides is offered as a challenge. Until now the children have only used the numbers in the equations, canceling or combining them. Trish introduces a new strategy — subtracting the same number from both sides. Subtracting six from each side in the third problem produces the fourth. As a member of the community, Trish offers the possibility for consideration. This is very different from telling children a strategy and asking them all to use it.

Pair talk invites children to reflect more deeply.

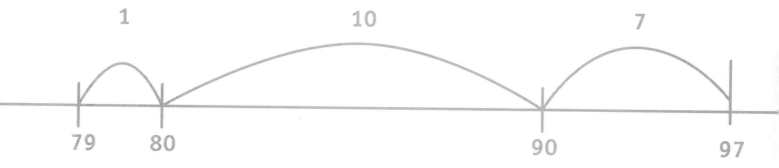

The Open Number Line

As described in the earlier section of this resource, an open number line is just an empty line used to record children's computation strategies. Whereas cubes with the support of the five-structure were used in the previous section, here they are no longer provided. Now children are encouraged to consider the operations mentally. Representations on a number line develop a sense of "number space" where proximity and distance can be examined.

Compensation, Equivalence, Moving to a Landmark

This string of related problems for double-digit addition encourages children to decompose numbers, compensating to make equivalent expressions. Do one problem at a time, recording children's strategies on the open number line. Invite children to comment on the representations and to share alternative strategies. When children begin to make use of the related problems as you progress through the string, invite a discussion on how helpful that can be. Suggest that children try to make problems into friendlier ones, as mathematicians do. At the end of the string, you might want to make signs of the important strategies discussed and post them on a strategy wall. Use children's own words, such as "Give and take" or "Use friendly numbers."

$$58 + 22$$

$$60 + 20$$

$$30 + 50$$

$$28 + 52$$

$$32 + 48$$

$$33 + 47$$

$$98 + 42$$

$$97 + 34$$

Behind the Numbers: How the String was Crafted

The first several problems in this string are all related in ways that will support and encourage children to think about equivalent expressions. The first six problems in the string are clustered into pairs and all six have the same answer. If children have not noticed the relationships after the sixth problem, point out that several of the answers are the same and discuss why that is happening. Ask which problem was the easiest to do. Represent the problems on the number line and discuss the strategy of taking from one number and giving to the other, so that the total stays the same — compensation. Here children are beginning to use the number line as a tool to think with. Once children understand the compensation strategy, encourage them to use it to make the last two problems friendlier. For example, 98 + 42 becomes an easy problem to solve when children realize it is equivalent to 100 + 40. For additional support, see the related strings that follow—C2 and C3.

Paul (the teacher): OK. Lots of nice strategies so far. Here's the next one…32 + 48. Let me know with thumbs-up when you are ready for discussion. *(After a few moments with several thumbs up.)* Rosa, Marianne, Harry, your thumbs aren't up yet. Do you need more time? *(They nod, and Paul waits another minute.)* OK, Rosa, what is your strategy?

Rosa: I took 8 off the 48 and I gave it to the 32. That got me to 40, and then another 40.

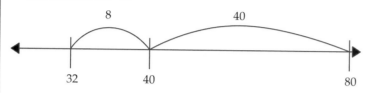

Paul: *(Drawing a representation of her strategy on an open number line.)* Comments or questions for Rosa? Do you agree with her? Marianne?

Marianne: I agree. Her way works. But my way was different.

Paul: Share your way.

Marianne: I took 2 off of 32 and gave it to 48, because 50 is nicer for me.

Paul: So you added that 2 to 48? Let me draw that.

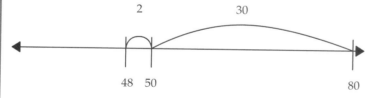

Paul: Seems we can make a lot of equivalent problems here. Rosa, you made 32 + 48 into 40 + 40, and Marianne, you made it into 30 + 50…and these are all 80?

Sam: And all the others, too. Look! All the answers are 80 so far!

Paul: Oh, wow! Look at that. Does everyone see what Sam has noticed? *(Several children comment: "Oh yeah! I know, I saw it, too," etc.)* Why did that happen? I did different problems, didn't I?

Sam: Yeah, but it's like we're giving and taking.

Paul: Giving and taking…Talk to the person next to you about Sam's idea. What does he mean, "giving and taking?" *(After pair talk.)* Shelley?

continued on next page

Author's Notes

The thumbs-up signal lets Paul know how much think time to provide. It also implies that thinking is cherished in this community.

Representing the strategy on the open number line provides a focus for reflection and discussion. Over time, the model will become a tool for the learners to use to think with — for now, Paul uses it simply to represent the steps.

Alternative strategies are valued.

Children are encouraged to look for patterns as they do minilesson strings.

The focus now shifts to justifying the strategy. Mathematicians must justify their actions to the community. Over time, justifying will evolve into formal proving.

continued from previous page

Shelley: It's like if your mom has 48 dollars and your dad has 32. If your mom gives your dad 8 dollars, now it's 40 and 40. Together they have 80, but they did before, too. If your dad gave your mom 2 dollars, she would have 50 and he would have 30. But together it's still 80.

Paul: This is a pretty neat strategy then, isn't it? We could use it to make messy problems friendly. Like Marianne said…she likes 50 and 48 was close. Rosa liked 40 and 40. That's a nice double. I've got three more problems in my string. Let's see if this strategy is helpful with them.

String · C2

Compensation, Equivalence, Moving to a Landmark

See C1 for details (page 35).

47 + 23

50 + 20

40 + 30

37 + 33

43 + 27

45 + 25

87 + 43

98 + 43

String · C3

Compensation, Equivalence, Moving to a Landmark

See C1 for details (page 35).

46 + 34

50 + 30

40 + 40

47 + 33

43 + 37

45 + 35

79 + 21

89 + 22

Keeping One Number Whole and Taking Leaps of Ten

This string of related problems is designed to encourage children to keep one number whole and take leaps of ten. Do one problem at a time and record children's strategies on the open number line, inviting children to comment on the representations. If you notice children beginning to make use of tens, discuss why this strategy is helpful. If the class agrees that it is a useful strategy for addition, you might want to make a sign about this and post it on a strategy wall. Use children's own words, such as "Take jumps of ten."

$$26 + 10$$
$$26 + 12$$
$$26 + 22$$
$$44 + 30$$
$$44 + 39$$
$$57 + 39$$

Behind the Numbers: How the String was Crafted

This string is designed to encourage children to keep one number whole and to take leaps of ten. The first problem provides the support for this strategy. The value of the expression in the second problem is just 2 greater than the first, and can be drawn right onto the representation of the first. The third problem requires another jump of 10 beyond the second expression. The fourth problem provides the support for the fifth, which has a value 9 greater than the fourth. This fifth problem also provides an opening for children to add 40 and subtract 1. The last problem has no helper problem provided, so children have to think about how to make the problem friendly. For additional support, see the related strings that follow—C5 and C6.

A Portion of the Minilesson

Julie (the teacher): So let's warm up with a string. Here's the first one, 26 + 10. Show me with a thumbs-up when you are ready. *(Most thumbs go up right away.)* Wow, I guess that was an easy one! Shari?

Shari: It's 36. I just knew it!

Julie: So adding ten is easy, isn't it? Maybe that is something to keep in mind as we do this string today. Here's the next one, 26 + 12. While you're thinking, let me get Shari's strategy on the open number line.

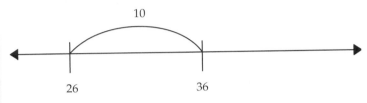

Carlos: You just add 2 more.

Julie: Oh, you used the first problem? You all know me with my strings, now, don't you? You are looking for relationships. Great. OK, let me add the 2 to Shari's line.

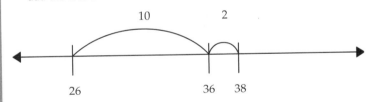

Julie: So adding 12 was easy because you made it 10 + 2. Did anyone have a different way?

Sophie: I was counting. But I like Carlos' way. That was fast.

Julie: It was, wasn't it? How about this one: 26 + 22. There are probably lots of ways, but let's see if we can think of fast ways, as Carlos did before.

Inside One Classroom

Author's Notes

Julie anticipated that this first problem would be easy. It is in the string only to provide support for the later problems and to suggest its use as a potential helper. Because it is easy there is no need to ask for a variety of solutions, or to have much discussion. Sometimes, asking for other ways to solve a problem when no other ways have been used makes children come up with a variety of strategies (many of them very tedious) just to please the teacher. On the other hand, when problems are difficult and several strategies have been tried, it is very important to explore them.

By adding on to the previous number line, Julie helps the children envision the relationship.

Efficiency is valued.

String · C5

Keeping One Number Whole and Taking Leaps of Ten

See C4 for details (page 38).

37 + 10

37 + 12

37 + 32

46 + 30

46 + 39

46 + 31

54 + 29

String · C6

Keeping One Number Whole and Taking Leaps of Ten

See C4 for details (page 38).

10 + 34

12 + 34

32 + 34

30 + 49

39 + 49

49 + 31

58 + 39

String · C7

Keeping One Number Whole, Moving to a Landmark and Then Taking Leaps of Ten

This string of related problems encourages children to continue to explore the addition strategy of using leaps of ten, but it extends that strategy to include decomposing an addend to get to a landmark number. As before, do one problem at a time. If you notice children beginning to make use of landmark numbers as you progress through the string, invite a discussion on how helpful that can be. If the class comes to a consensus that this is indeed a helpful strategy, you might want to make a sign about this and post it on your strategy wall, "Keep one number whole and move to a landmark."

$$59 + 1$$
$$59 + 11$$
$$48 + 12$$
$$58 + 22$$
$$38 + 6$$
$$38 + 26$$
$$59 + 33$$

Behind the Numbers: How the String was Crafted

Since the string is designed to encourage keeping one number whole and decomposing the other addend to get to a landmark number, the first problem is used to provide support. The value of the expression in the second problem is just 10 more than the first. The third problem has no helper problem, but 50 is a strong landmark for children and they may think to use the 2 (from the 12) to get there. If no one decomposes the 12 to get to 50, you might wonder aloud if that strategy would have worked and show it. The fourth problem allows children to test the strategy that is the focus of the string again. The fifth and sixth problems are paired to continue supporting the strategy, although this time, the 6—a single-digit number—has to be decomposed. The last problem in the string requires children to make their own equivalent problem, such as 60 + 30 + 2 or 60 + 32. For additional support, see the related strings that follow—C8 and C9.

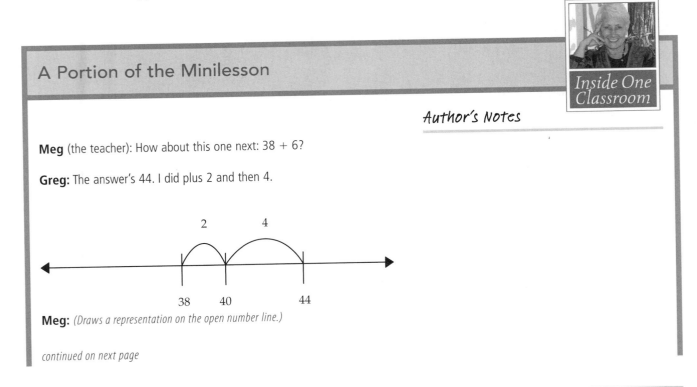

A Portion of the Minilesson

Inside One Classroom

Author's Notes

Meg (the teacher): How about this one next: 38 + 6?

Greg: The answer's 44. I did plus 2 and then 4.

Meg: *(Draws a representation on the open number line.)*

continued on next page

continued from previous page

Erin, I see you writing that one down. *(Erin has written the problem down vertically and regrouped.)*

Erin: I did 8 and 6. I wrote down the 4 and carried a 1. Then I did 1 + 3. My mom showed me this way.

Meg: OK. Let's try to figure out why it works. What is that "1" that you said you carried? *(Erin looks puzzled.)*

Carlos: It's a ten, I think, because 10 + 4 is 14.

Meg: Yes. So did Erin do 30 + 14? Is it a ten, Erin? *(Erin still looks puzzled.)* Erin, do you understand what Greg did before?

Erin: Yes. He did 2 to get to 40 and then 4 more. That is 6.

Often parents or siblings teach the standard algorithm before the child has a deep enough understanding of place value to understand it. The algorithm should not be avoided; it is a helpful strategy when numbers are large, messy, or numerous, such as the case of having to add a long column of numbers. The algorithm should not need to be used with simple problems like 38 + 6. Meg encourages Erin to make sense of the problem since she does not appear to understand the procedures in the standard algorithm.

Erin can easily add 6 and 20 onto 38 with understanding when allowed to decompose in her own way.

String · C8

Keeping One Number Whole, Moving to a Landmark and Then Taking Leaps of Ten

See C7 for details (page 40).

48 + 2

48 + 12

47 + 13

47 + 14

49 + 7

49 + 37

69 + 24

String · C9

Keeping One Number Whole, Moving to a Landmark and Then Taking Leaps of Ten

See C7 for details (page 40).

57 + 3

57 + 13

98 + 12

98 + 22

46 + 8

46 + 28

79 + 23

Partial Sums, Splitting, Expanded Notation

This string of related problems encourages children to use expanded notation and make partial sums. Sometimes this strategy is termed *splitting* since the addends are split by column, making use of expanded notation. Using expanded notation is easier for children than the standard algorithm because place value requires children to think multiplicatively. Rather than thinking of 33 as 30 + 3 (as in expanded notation), the algorithm requires thinking of 33 as $(3 \times 10) + 3$.

As always, do one problem at a time. If the class comes to a consensus that this is indeed a helpful strategy, you might want to make a sign about this and add it to your strategy wall.

$$3 + 5$$
$$50 + 10$$
$$53 + 15$$
$$40 + 20$$
$$48 + 22$$
$$6 + 6$$
$$36 + 16$$
$$33 + 26$$

Behind the Numbers: How the String was Crafted

Since the string is designed to encourage splitting, it begins with two problems that can be used to solve the third. The fourth and fifth problems are a pair, but here the children need to make the other helper problem (8 + 2) themselves. This is also the case with the next two problems; the children will need to make the helper problem (30 + 10). The last problem in the string requires children to decompose the addends. For additional support, see the related strings that follow—C11 and C12.

Inside One Classroom

A Portion of the Minilesson

Author's Notes

Hildy (the teacher): How about this one next: 48 + 22?

José: I used the problem before it. I used 40 + 20. Then it's 10 more.

continued on next page

continued from previous page

Hildy: *(Draws a representation on the open number line.)*

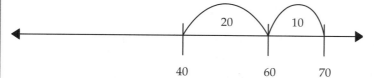

So you split the 48 and the 22.

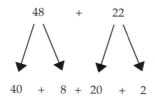

Did anyone do it a different way?

Jaleelah: I kept the 48 whole and added 2, then 20.

Hildy: So you made the problem into 50 + 20. Let me draw that on the number line.

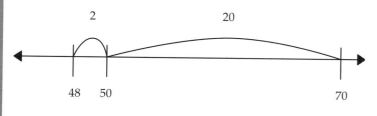

Hildy represents splitting two ways: on the number line, but also with arrows to show where the pieces have come from. Although splitting is a common strategy that children construct, it is not the most efficient since it results in several numbers to keep in mind. The arrows help children remember where the numbers came from.

Alternative strategies are accepted and encouraged. In fact, this strategy is very efficient given the numbers (48 is close to a landmark), and keeping one number whole here makes the problem easy to do mentally.

String · C11

Partial Sums, Splitting, Expanded Notation

See C10 for details (page 43).

4 + 6

40 + 30

44 + 36

50 + 30

57 + 33

7 + 7

37 + 27

33 + 27

62 + 22

Behind the Numbers: How the String was Crafted

Since the string is designed to encourage splitting, it begins with two problems that can be used to solve the third. The fourth and fifth problems are a pair, but here the children need to make the other helper problem (7 + 3) themselves. The next problem provides the support of one partial sum for the subsequent problem, but the children will need to make the helper (30 + 20). The last problem in the string requires them to decompose both addends themselves.

String · C12

Partial Sums, Splitting, Expanded Notation

See C10 for details (page 43).

3 + 6

50 + 40

56 + 43

60 + 30

62 + 37

8 + 8

48 + 28

53 + 32

String · C13

Part-Whole Relations
(Connecting Addition and Subtraction), Adding On vs. Removing

This string of related problems highlights the strategies of counting back when numbers are far apart on the number line, and counting on when numbers are close together. Do one problem at a time and record children's strategies on the open number line, inviting them to comment on the representations. If you notice that children are varying their strategies, invite a discussion on why they count back sometimes and count on at other times. If the class comes to a consensus that it is easier to count on when numbers are close together on the number line and to count back when they are far apart, you might want to make a sign about this and post it on your strategy wall. The big idea that underlies this strategy is the connection between addition and subtraction—how the parts are related to the whole.

$$82 - 6$$
$$64 - 59$$
$$56 - 8$$
$$94 - 91$$
$$132 - 6$$
$$135 - 13$$
$$132 - 128$$
$$135 - 122$$

Behind the Numbers: How the String was Crafted

The problems in the string were chosen to vary the situations when the numbers are close together and when they are far apart. Some of the problems are related, such as $132 - 6 = 128$ and $132 - 128 = 6$. By juxtaposing related problems, you guarantee a discussion of the relationship of addition to subtraction, how the parts are related to the whole, and how when numbers are close together it is easier to think of subtraction as difference and just add onto the subtrahend. On the other hand, when the numbers are far apart, it may be easier to think of subtraction as removing the subtrahend. For additional support, see the related strings that follow—C14 and C15.

A Portion of the Minilesson

Inside One Classroom

Author's Notes

Michael (the teacher): Here's the first warm-up problem: 82 − 6. Thumbs-up when you have an answer. Mario?

Mario: 76. I counted back: 81, 80, 79, 78. 77, 76.

Michael: *(Draws the following representation of Mario's strategy.)*

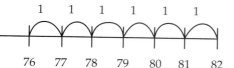

Mario's strategy is represented in small jumps. Michael presses for a more efficient strategy.

Does everyone agree with Mario? *(No disagreement is apparent.)* Does anyone have a way to do that one with fewer steps? Your way works, Mario, but it was a lot of counting that you needed to keep track of. Emmy?

continued on next page

continued from previous page

Emmy: I did a jump of 2 and then 4.

Michael: Let's see what that looks like on the number line. *(Using Mario's number line, Michael records Emmy's jumps in a different color.)*

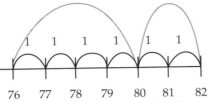

Representing the strategies on the same line allows the children to compare them.

What do you think, Mario? Does Emmy's way work? Saves a lot of counting, doesn't it? OK, let's go on to the next problem, 64 − 59. Show me with thumbs-up when you are ready. Susie.

Susie: It's 5. I just thought of the difference. It's 1 to get to 60, then 4 more.

Michael: Nice. You used a landmark number to help, too, like Emmy. Let me record your strategy.

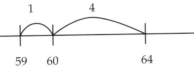

Here's the next one, 56 − 8. Mario, want to try taking leaps? What's a nice landmark number here?

Michael pulls Mario into the conversation and encourages him to consider taking larger steps.

Mario: 50. I could do a jump of 6 to get there, then…

Michael: How many more do you need to take away? You want to take 8 away altogether.

Mario: I think it's 2 more.

Michael: I'll make a picture. Let's be sure.

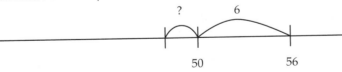

Mario: It is 2, because 6 + 2 is 8. *(Michael draws the following to complete the problem:)*

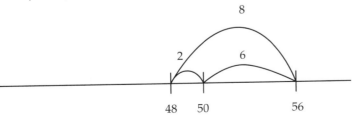

continued on next page

continued from previous page

Michael: So 48. I have another question. Seems like sometimes we are going forward, adding, and other times we are going backward. Talk to the person next to you about this. Why switch your strategy? *(Allows a few minutes of pair talk.)*

Manuel: When the numbers are close together, it is easier to add up. When they are far apart, like 56 and 8, it's easier to go back.

Michael: How many of you agree with Manuel? Let's think about this as we continue with our string. If we agree at the end, we can make a sign and post it on our strategy wall.

Although Michael is encouraging the use of landmark numbers, he is also focused on the connection between addition and subtraction. He questions the children to focus reflection on when it might be helpful to think of subtraction as difference (and thus add on) and when it might be easier to remove the subtrahend (and thus count back).

String · C14

Part-Whole Relations (Connecting Addition and Subtraction), Adding On vs. Removing

See C13 for details (page 45).

$$63 - 4$$
$$63 - 59$$
$$101 - 5$$
$$101 - 96$$
$$121 - 5$$
$$121 - 118$$
$$1001 - 999$$
$$1001 - 5$$

String · C15

Part-Whole Relations (Connecting Addition and Subtraction), Adding On vs. Removing

See C13 for details (page 45).

$$46 - 7$$
$$46 - 39$$
$$73 - 6$$
$$73 - 69$$
$$103 - 5$$
$$103 - 97$$
$$2003 - 1998$$
$$2003 - 4$$

Keeping One Number Whole and Taking Leaps of One Hundred

This string of related problems is designed to encourage children to keep one number whole and take leaps of one hundred first. Do one problem at a time and record children's strategies on the open number line, inviting them to comment on the representations. If you notice children beginning to make use of the hundreds, discuss why this strategy is helpful. If the class agrees that it is a useful strategy for addition, you might want to make a sign about this and post it on a strategy wall. Use children's own words, such as "Take big jumps first."

$$326 + 100$$
$$326 + 120$$
$$326 + 122$$
$$404 + 300$$
$$404 + 339$$
$$257 + 319$$

Behind the Numbers: How the String was Crafted

Since the string is designed to encourage children to keep one number whole and to take leaps of one hundred the first problem lays the terrain for this strategy. The value of the second expression is 20 greater than the value of the first, and can be drawn onto the representation of the first. The third problem requires just another jump of 2 beyond the second. The fourth problem lays the terrain for the fifth, the sum of which is just 39 greater than the fourth. Here, perhaps some children will think to add 40 and remove 1. The last problem has no helper problem provided, so children have to think about how to make the problem friendly. For additional support, see the related strings that follow—C17 and C18.

A Portion of the Minilesson

Inside One Classroom

Michael (the teacher): So let's warm up with a string. Here's the first one: 326 + 100. Show me with thumbs-up when you are ready. *(Most thumbs go up right away.)* Wow, I guess that was an easy one! Shari?

Shari: The answer's 426. I just knew it!

continued on next page

Author's Notes

Michael anticipated that this first problem would be easy. It is in the string only to provide support for the later problems and to suggest its potential use as a helper. Because it is easy, there is no need to ask for a variety of solutions or to have much discussion. Sometimes, asking for other ways to solve a problem when no one has used other ways makes children come up with a variety (many of them very tedious) just to please the teacher.

continued from previous page

Michael: So adding hundreds is easy, isn't it? Maybe that's something to keep in mind as we do this string. Here's the next one: 326 + 120. While you're thinking, let me get Shari's strategy on the open number line.

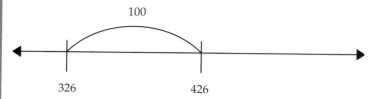

Carlos: You just add twenty more.

Michael: Oh, you used the first problem? You're looking for relationships. Great. Let me add the 20 to Shari's line.

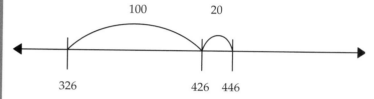

So adding 120 was easy because you made it 100 + 20. Did anyone have a different way?

Sophie: I was going to put 4 onto 326. But I like Carlos' way. That was fast.

Michael: It was, wasn't it? How about this one: 326 + 122. There are probably lots of ways, but let's see if we can think of fast ways, like Carlos did before.

On the other hand, when problems are difficult and several strategies have been tried, it is very important to explore them.

By adding on to the previous number line, Michael helps the children envision the relationship.

By providing related problems, Michael encourages children to look to the numbers first.

String · C17

Keeping One Number Whole and Taking Leaps of One Hundred

See C16 for details (page 49).

123 + 100

123 + 130

123 + 132

407 + 400

407 + 429

412 + 319

String · C18

Keeping One Number Whole and Taking Leaps of One Hundred

See C16 for details (page 49).

$$234 + 200$$
$$234 + 240$$
$$234 + 245$$
$$519 + 300$$
$$519 + 312$$
$$623 + 339$$

String · C19

Removing Groups of Ten and Adjusting

This string of related problems is designed to encourage children to keep one number whole, take leaps of ten, and adjust as needed at the end—to use an equivalent form to simplify the problem. For example, to subtract 19 one might use $-20 + 1$. Do one problem at a time and record children's strategies on the open number line, inviting them to comment on the representations. If you notice children making use of equivalent forms, discuss why this strategy is helpful. If the class agrees that it is a useful strategy for subtraction, you might want to make a sign about this and post it on a strategy wall. Use children's own words, such as "Take jumps of ten first then adjust."

$$26 - 10$$
$$26 - 9$$
$$43 - 20$$
$$43 - 19$$
$$63 - 39$$
$$57 - 39$$

Behind the Numbers: How the String was Crafted

Since the string is designed to encourage children to keep one number whole and to take leaps of ten, the first problem lays the terrain for this strategy. The difference of the second problem is 1 less than the first, and is paired with the first to encourage children to simply adjust by adding 1 back in. The third and fourth problems are paired in a similar way. The fifth and sixth problems require children to make their own helper problems, so children have to think about how to make the problems friendly. If you want to lengthen this string, make more problems in which the subtrahend has 8 or 9 ones. For additional support, see the related strings that follow—C20 through C24.

Inside One Classroom

Hildy (the teacher): So let's warm up with a string. Here's the first one: 26 − 10. Show me with thumbs-up when you are ready. *(Most thumbs go up right away.)* Wow, I guess that was an easy one! Lisa?

Lisa: It's 16. I just knew it!

Hildy: So subtracting a ten is easy, isn't it? Maybe that's something to keep in mind as we do this string. Here's next one: 26 − 9. While you're thinking, let me get Lisa's strategy on the open number line. I wonder if there is a way to use it for this problem.

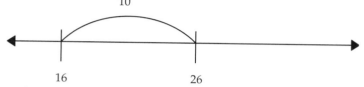

Keshawn: You just add 1 back.

Hildy: Oh, you found a way to use the first problem, Keshawn. What a great strategy! Turn to the person next to you and talk about what Keshawn did. *(After a few minutes of pair talk.)* Deron?

Deron: Well, 9 is just 1 away from 10. So you have to add it back.

Hildy: So he thought of 9 as 10 − 1, didn't he? I'll draw what he said on Lisa's number line.

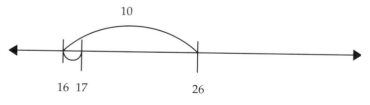

Author's Notes

Hildy anticipated that this first problem would be easy. It is in the string only to provide support for the later problems and to suggest its potential use as a helper. Because it is easy, there is no need to ask for a variety of solutions, or to have much discussion. Sometimes, asking for other ways to solve a problem when no one has used other ways makes children come up with a variety (many of them very tedious) just to please the teacher. On the other hand, when problems are difficult and several strategies have been tried, it is very important to explore them. When working through the problems, be sure to be open to the use of more than one strategy.

By adding on to the previous number line, Hildy helps the children envision the relationship.

String · C20

Removing Groups of Ten and Adjusting

See C19 for details (page 51).

$$37 - 10$$
$$37 - 9$$
$$63 - 20$$
$$63 - 19$$
$$54 - 39$$
$$83 - 29$$

String · C21

Removing Groups of Ten and Adjusting

See C19 for details (page 51).

$$43 - 20$$
$$43 - 19$$
$$47 - 30$$
$$47 - 39$$
$$52 - 19$$
$$83 - 39$$

String · C22

Removing Groups of Ten and Adjusting

See C19 for details (page 51).

$$156 - 10$$
$$156 - 9$$
$$147 - 20$$
$$147 - 19$$
$$122 - 40$$
$$122 - 39$$
$$181 - 49$$

String · C23

Removing Groups of Ten and Adjusting

See C19 for details (page 51).

$$143 - 10$$
$$143 - 9$$
$$143 - 20$$
$$143 - 19$$
$$143 - 21$$
$$157 - 50$$
$$157 - 49$$
$$192 - 59$$

String · C24

Removing Groups of Ten and Adjusting

See C19 for details (page 51).

$$137 - 10$$
$$137 - 9$$
$$137 - 20$$
$$137 - 19$$
$$137 - 21$$
$$153 - 40$$
$$153 - 39$$
$$172 - 69$$

String · C25

Constant Difference, Equivalence

This string of related problems encourages learners to explore constant difference—making problems friendlier by using an equivalent expression, for example using $70 - 35$ to solve $71 - 36$. Do one problem at a time and record children's strategies on the open number line, inviting them to comment on the representations and to share alternative strategies. If you notice children beginning to make use of the related problems, invite a discussion of how helpful that can be and how thinking about subtraction as age differences and just sliding up and down the number line might make it easy. Suggest that children try to make problems into friendlier ones, as mathematicians do. If the class comes to a consensus that this is a helpful strategy, you might want to make a sign about this and post it on your wall of "Helpful Subtraction Strategies."

$$70 - 35$$
$$71 - 36$$
$$72 - 37$$
$$69 - 34$$
$$75 - 40$$
$$152 - 49$$
$$174 - 59$$

Behind the Numbers: How the String was Crafted

The first five problems in the string are all related in ways that will support and encourage children to think about constant difference. If they have not noticed the relationships after the fifth problem, introduce more equivalent problems, such as $68 - 33$, $73 - 38$, and $74 - 39$. Once the fact that the answers are all the same becomes apparent, discuss why that is happening. When discussing why the constant difference strategy works, it is helpful to represent the problems on the number line as difference (not as removal). The figures below show subtraction as difference and subtraction as removal represented on the number line for the problem $71 - 36$.

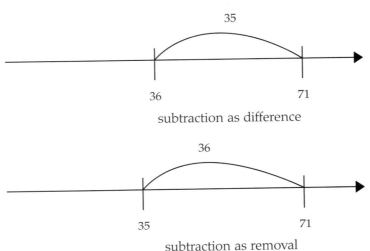

subtraction as difference

subtraction as removal

Explore equivalent expressions on the number line and discuss how the problems are just sliding up and down, while the difference is staying the same. You can also put the numbers in the context of age differences — for example, "My mother is 70 and I am 35, and when I am 36, she will be 71." Once children understand the strategy, encourage them to use it to make the last two problems friendly. For example, $152 - 49$ becomes an easy problem to solve when children realize it is equivalent to $153 - 50$. For additional support, see the related strings that follow—C26 through C30.

String · C26

Constant Difference, Equivalence

See C25 for details (page 54).

$$60 - 45$$
$$61 - 46$$
$$59 - 44$$
$$62 - 47$$
$$107 - 39$$
$$201 - 79$$
$$1001 - 899$$

String · C27

Constant Difference, Equivalence

See C25 for details (page 54).

$$80 - 25$$
$$81 - 26$$
$$82 - 27$$
$$79 - 24$$
$$140 - 98$$
$$163 - 59$$
$$184 - 78$$

String · C28

Constant Difference, Equivalence

See C25 for details (page 54).

$$90 - 40$$
$$91 - 39$$
$$91 - 41$$
$$52 - 38$$
$$54 - 40$$
$$63 - 38$$
$$172 - 49$$
$$174 - 89$$

Behind the Numbers: How the String was Crafted

The first three problems in the string are designed to support a discussion on constant difference. The first problem is easy; the second may cause children to make errors (91 is an increase of 1, while 39 is a decrease of 1, so the answer is 52, not 50). It has been placed here deliberately to give you a chance to represent the errors on the number line and explore constant difference once again. The third problem, when contrasted with the second, will help refocus the conversation on what is happening. The last three problems in the string require children to make their own helper problems.

String · C29

Constant Difference, Equivalence

See C25 for details (page 54).

$$85 - 45$$
$$79 + 21$$
$$86 - 44$$
$$95 - 55$$
$$143 - 39$$
$$234 - 29$$

Behind the Numbers: How the String was Crafted

The first four problems in the string are designed to support a discussion on constant difference. The first one is easy. The second addition problem is likely to generate a compensation strategy: $79 + 21 = 80 + 20$. Children may then try to use compensation for subtraction in the third problem making $90 - 40$, only to discover that it doesn't work. This structure in the design of the string has been used deliberately to give you a chance to represent the errors on the number line and discuss constant difference once again. The third problem, when contrasted with the fourth, will help refocus the conversation on what is happening. The last two problems in the string require children to make their own helper problems.

String · C30

Constant Difference, Equivalence

See C25 for details (page 54).

178 + 22

89 − 41

90 − 42

100 − 52

98 − 50

143 − 39

234 − 29

String · C31

Assessment

This mental math minilesson includes many problems that can be made easier with constant difference; however, that is not the focus. The string is not organized in a specific fashion to support one strategy over another. It is designed simply as an assessment tool. As before, do one problem at a time and record children's strategies on the open number line, inviting children to comment on the representations and to share alternative strategies. Note the variety of strategies your students use here. This is a good chance to assess the variety they have in their toolboxes, and whether they are able to choose strategies that make the computation efficient.

2006 − 1999

1999 − 1987

1992 − 8

52 − 6

54 − 29

63 − 38

172 − 45

174 − 89

Behind the Numbers: How the String was Crafted

The problems in this string are not related; however, the numbers have been chosen carefully in that several strategies can be used to make the problems easy. For example, the first problem might be solved with constant difference (2007 − 2000 = 2006 − 1999) or by adding on from the subtrahend. Using pencil and paper and the standard regrouping algorithm here would show a lack of numeracy. This string provides a good chance to notice and assess the subtraction strategies your students have in their toolboxes. Do they vary adding on and removing, take jumps of ten back and adjust, split, use landmarks, and make use of equivalent expressions? C32 provides another opportunity to assess strategies.

String · C32

Assessment

See C31 for details (page 58).

$$102 - 5$$
$$102 - 97$$
$$1003 - 5$$
$$1003 - 997$$
$$152 - 49$$
$$152 - 3$$
$$10,002 - 5$$
$$10,002 - 9999$$

The Money Model

Money can be a helpful model for addition and subtraction. Quarters, nickels, and dimes can be used to develop familiarity and fluency with landmark numbers. Quantities can also be composed, decomposed, and exchanged using the context of coins, to encourage equivalence and computation strategies such as adding or removing tens, hundreds, and other landmarks. The primary focus of this section is early algebra with an emphasis on exchange, equivalence, and variation.

Equivalence, Exchange

This mental math minilesson uses a format like the game "twenty questions" to provide children with opportunities to think about equivalence. There are two problems, each using coins totaling 50 cents. Do one problem at a time. Place the coins in your closed palm without allowing children to identify them. Announce that the total value of the coins in your hand is 50 cents. Have children take turns asking questions that can be answered only by yes or no, such as "Do you have a quarter?" or "Do you have two dimes?" (If you have only one dime in your hand, the answer would be no; if the question is "Do you have any dimes?" the answer would be yes.) Record the questions and answers on a chart or chalkboard. Keep track of the number of questions it takes for the class to determine the exact coins you're holding, clarifying that the limit is 20. Notice children who are beginning to ask questions based on anticipating equivalence; for example, since the target is 50 cents and if pennies and nickels have been ruled out, only two possibilities exist: two quarters or five dimes. Have children share the thinking underlying their questions.

Note: If you have a linguistically diverse classroom or many children for whom English is not their first language, you may need to explicitly discuss different wording in the questions. For example, the difference between "Do you have a quarter?" and "Do you have one quarter?" may need some elaboration. See D2 for additional support.

3 dimes, 4 nickels

1 quarter, 5 nickels

Behind the Numbers: How the String was Crafted

The coins have been carefully chosen to encourage children to consider substitution and equivalence. The first problem has no quarters. Children will probably ask about quarters first since this coin has the greatest value. Once quarters and pennies are ruled out, children only need to consider the combinations of dimes and nickels that are possible. The second problem has one quarter; once this is established, children only need to consider ways to make 25 cents. This logic, however, may still be out of reach for many children. You should therefore elicit the logic underlying their questioning. The limited number of possible questions (twenty) is an important constraint in this activity as it pushes children to consider what makes a good question. After the children solve the two problems, write them in equation form, using circles to represent the coins: $3 \textcircled{10} + 4 \textcircled{5} = 1 \textcircled{25} + 5 \textcircled{5}$. Children will need to examine what you might have exchanged as you went from the first problem to the second. Encourage them to examine the equation by decomposing the numbers and exchanging equivalent amounts, rather than adding to find the totals.

Trish (the teacher): So you figured out what coins I had in my hand, both times…and you did it with fewer than twenty questions. Wow! Nice job. You are getting good at this! So let me write an equation for the two problems. *(Writes:)*

$$3\,\textcircled{10} + 4\,\textcircled{5} = 1\,\textcircled{25} + 5\,\textcircled{5}$$

Is this a true statement?

Juanita: Yes, because 30, that's 3 dimes, and 20 cents more is 50. On the other side is 25 and 25. That's 50, too. So 50 equals 50. You had 50 cents both times.

Trish: So one way is to do all the arithmetic. That convinces us, doesn't it? I wonder…are there other ways we could know that the two sides of the equation are equal, too…without doing all the arithmetic? Maria?

Maria: I know a dime is 2 nickels…and a quarter is 2 dimes and a nickel.

Trish: *(Writes:)*

$$3\,\textcircled{10} + 4\,\textcircled{5} \; ? \; 1\,\textcircled{25} + 5\,\textcircled{5}$$

$$1\,\textcircled{10} = 2\,\textcircled{5}$$

$$1\,\textcircled{25} = 2\,\textcircled{10} + 1\,\textcircled{5}$$

Let's look at what Maria said so far. Don't tell us yet how that helped you, Maria. Let's see if we can figure out what you did next. Turn to the person next to you and talk about Maria's thinking so far, and then discuss what you think she will say next. *(After some pair talk, the conversation resumes.)* Carlos? What did you and Katie talk about?

Carlos: She made it the same. We agree, a dime is 2 nickels, and a quarter is 2 dimes and a nickel. So she can trade and rearrange some more.

Trish: Is that how you knew, Maria?

Maria: Yep. Both sides have a quarter and 5 nickels. *(Trish writes Maria's actions to the right. To the left she writes the resulting equations:)*

$$1\,\textcircled{25} + 5\,\textcircled{5} = 2\,\textcircled{10} + 1\,\textcircled{5} + 5\,\textcircled{5} \quad \Big| \quad \text{Trade}$$

$$1\,\textcircled{25} + 5\,\textcircled{5} = 2\,\textcircled{10} + 2\,\textcircled{5} + 4\,\textcircled{5} \quad \Big| \quad \text{Rearrange}$$

$$1\,\textcircled{25} + 5\,\textcircled{5} = 3\,\textcircled{10} + 4\,\textcircled{5} \quad \Big| \quad \text{Trade}$$

Author's Notes

The context of coins helps children realize the meaning of what they are doing as they seek to establish equivalence.

Trish challenges the children to consider the expressions as objects.

Trish writes the givens — the true statements underlying Maria's argument. By encouraging the whole community to consider what Maria's next steps might be, Trish enables others to develop similar arguments.

Pair talk provides reflection time and implicitly says that we are a community engaged in thinking. We consider each other's ideas.

By writing down Maria's actions on the right, Trish introduces two-column proofs. This modeling also leaves a visible representation of Maria's thinking for others to read and reflect on. Reading others' mathematics, following their arguments, and determining if the arguments hold is an important part of what mathematicians do.

Equivalence, Exchange

See D1 for details (page 61).

2 dimes, 10 pennies, 4 nickels

15 pennies, 2 nickels, 1 quarter

Behind the Numbers: How the String was Crafted

The coins have been chosen to encourage children to consider exchanges and equivalence. The first problem has no quarters and ten pennies. Notice whether children ask about pennies in multiples of five. Those who ask if you have six pennies, or two, are not yet able to understand that these numbers of coins are impossible if the total is 50 cents. The second problem encourages children to realize that even though the total is the same as in the first problem, the coins are different. When the equation is written at the end, children will need to discuss what coins you must have exchanged. Here there are a variety of possibilities. For example, one possibility is that 2 dimes and 1 nickel have been exchanged for 1 quarter and another nickel has been exchanged for 5 pennies. Do not explain what you did. Instead, challenge children to consider different possibilities and to search for all of them.

Twenty Questions · D3

Equivalence, Variation

This mental math minilesson is similar to D1 and D2 but it introduces a foreign coin of unknown value to explore variation. Put coins in two bags; do not tell children the total value of the coins in each bag. Place one of the pictures of the foreign coins in each bag. Children work to establish whether the total value of coins in each bag is the same. Record coins as children determine them, using the appropriate relational sign ($<$, $>$, $=$) in the statement (as shown in Inside One Classroom on page 64). Have children share their thinking as they determine which sign is appropriate. As you proceed, record what the community knows for certain and ask children to determine the appropriate relational sign to compare the values. As each new determination is made, discuss whether or not to change the sign and how children know that their choice is correct. Announce that you have a foreign coin in each bag *after* they have determined all the other coins and think they are finished. Explain that although you don't know what the foreign coins are worth, you are certain that they are identical.

Problem #1

Bag #1: 1 quarter, 3 dimes, 4 nickels, 1 foreign coin (C)

Bag #2: 1 quarter, 2 dimes, 6 nickels, 1 foreign coin (C)

Problem #2

Bag #1: 1 quarter, 2 dimes, 4 nickels, 1 foreign coin (C)

Bag #2: 1 quarter, 2 dimes, 6 nickels, 1 foreign coin (C)

Behind the Numbers: How the String was Crafted

The foreign coin has been added to engage children in determining equivalence of expressions with a variable added. The value of the coin in U.S. money is unknown. For Problem #1, the value of the coins in Bag #1 equals that in Bag #2 without the foreign coin. Each bag contains the same type of foreign coin, C, so the bags contain equal values no matter what the foreign coin is worth.

The second problem is chosen to involve children in considering unequal values. Here, as long as each bag has the same type of foreign coin, the total values of the coins contained in the bags are unequal. Expect children to have a spirited discussion about the addition of the foreign coin. Some will say it is not possible to decide if the values in the bags are equal without knowing the value of the foreign coin. Children who are still adding values—doing all the arithmetic to determine which relational sign to use—will be especially resistant to accepting the idea that a determination can be made.

Inside One Classroom

A Portion of the Minilesson (Problem #1)

Author's Notes

Trish (the teacher): So far you have figured out that there is 1 quarter in each bag plus 2 dimes in this bag on the left. Let me write that down. What sign should I use so far?

Several voices: Greater than.

Trish challenges the children to consider the expressions as objects. Which is greater in value, or are they equivalent?

Trish: Why? Sam?

Sam: Well, the quarters are the same, but the bag on the left has 2 dimes.

Trish: OK. *(Writes:)*

$$1\,(25) + 2\,(10) > 1\,(25)$$

Do you have more questions for me?

continued on next page

continued from previous page

Juanita: Are there more than 2 dimes in the other bag?

Trish: Yes.

Kelly: Are there 3?

Trish: Exactly? *(Child nods.)* Yes. So let's write this down. Now you know the quarters and the dimes. Which sign do we need?

Trish checks for clarification and then represents the statement. She does not provide the sign. She requires the children to think and determine which sign should be used.

Juanita: You have to turn the sign around. Make it point to 1 quarter and 2 dimes.

Trish: OK. So here is what we have now. *(Writes:)*

$$1\,\text{(25)} + 2\,\text{(10)} < 1\,\text{(25)} + 3\,\text{(10)}$$

(Discussion continues until the following equation is determined and pennies are ruled out:)

$$1\,\text{(25)} + 2\,\text{(10)} + 6\,\text{(5)} = 1\,\text{(25)} + 3\,\text{(10)} + 4\,\text{(5)}$$

Trish: You think we are done now, don't you? Actually there is one more coin in each bag and it is the same type of coin in each bag.

Juanita: What is it?

Trish: I don't know what this type of coin is worth. They are foreign coins that I got a long time ago when I was traveling. I put one in each bag. Let's call it C for *coin* because we don't know what it's worth. Here's what we know so far. *(Writes:)*

The variable is introduced.

$$1\,\text{(25)} + 2\,\text{(10)} + 6\,\text{(5)} + C \ ? \ 1\,\text{(25)} + 3\,\text{(10)} + 4\,\text{(5)} + C$$

What sign should we use?

Sam: We can't do it if you don't tell us. How can we add it if we don't know what it is?

If children are still performing the operations, this problem seems impossible to work with. One of the biggest stumbling blocks for older students when they encounter algebra is that they do not have a strong sense of equivalence.

Trish: Do you have to add it?

Rosie: If it's a nickel, it's still equal.

Juanita: It works for a penny or a dime, too.

Trish encourages children to consider several numbers as a way of developing the idea of a variable.

Trish: Does it work for other numbers, too?

Keshawn: It works for any number, because it's the same in both bags.

Isaac: You don't have to know what it is. If it's the same coin and it's in both bags, you don't have to worry about it. It's the same on both sides so it's still the equal sign.

continued on next page

continued from previous page

Trish: Could C be any amount? Are Keshawn and Isaac right? Would this be true no matter what C is? *(Changes the question mark in the equation to an equal sign:)*

$$1\,\widehat{25} + 2\,\widehat{10} + 6\,\widehat{5} + C = 1\,\widehat{25} + 3\,\widehat{10} + 4\,\widehat{5} + C$$

Isaac: Yep.

Trish: Doesn't it matter what C is?

Michael: No. C could be any number. As long as you give both bags the same, it doesn't matter what the value of the C coin is.

Trish challenges the children to generalize. When they have constructed their own rules in the community, they use them to justify and prove their ideas.

String · D4

Partial Sums, Splitting, Standard Regrouping Algorithm

This string of related problems encourages children to make partial sums. Sometimes this strategy is termed *splitting* since the amounts are split by column, making use of expanded notation. Expanded notation is easier for children to work with than the standard algorithm, because place value requires children to think multiplicatively. Rather than thinking of 33 as 30 + 3 (expanded notation), the algorithm requires thinking of 33 as $(3 \times 10) + 3$. Money (dollars, dimes, and pennies) is a good model (or context) to use to develop the standard algorithms for addition and subtraction. The context can help children realize the worth of the columns (10 cents is also 1 dime) and provide a bridge from the use of splitting to the standard regrouping algorithms. As always, do one problem at a time.

3 pennies + 5 pennies

5 dimes + 1 dime

53 cents + 15 cents

40 + 20: How many dimes?

48 cents + 22 cents

6 + 6

36 + 16

33 + 26

42 + 18

Behind the Numbers: How the String was Crafted

Since the string is designed to encourage splitting initially, it begins with two problems that can be used to solve the third. The fourth and fifth problems are a pair. The question, *How many dimes?* provides a scaffold to regrouping. Cents is used in place of pennies to encourage children to consider how 53 cents might be 5 dimes and 3 pennies. In the next two problems the children will need to make the helper (30 + 10), or 3 dimes and 1 dime. The last two problems in the string require them to decompose the addends. For additional support, see the related strings that follow—D5 through D8.

String · D5

Partial Sums, Splitting, Standard Regrouping Algorithm

See D4 for details (page 66).

13 dimes + 5 pennies

12 dimes + 15 pennies

135 cents − 9 cents

135 cents − 16 cents

6 dimes + 10 cents: How many dimes?

7 dimes − 36 cents

90 cents − 26 cents

12 dimes + 3 cents

123 cents − 64 cents

132 cents − 49 cents

String · D6

Partial Sums, Splitting, Standard Regrouping Algorithm

See D4 for details (page 66).

18 dimes + 5 pennies

17 dimes + 15 pennies

185 cents − 9 cents

185 cents − 16 cents

5 dimes + 10 cents: How many dimes?

6 dimes − 36 cents

60 cents − 26 cents

12 dimes + 3 cents

123 cents − 64 cents

145 cents − 39 cents

String · D7

Partial Sums, Splitting, Standard Regrouping Algorithm

See D4 for details (page 66).

20 dimes + 8 pennies

19 dimes + 18 pennies

$2.08 − 16 cents

$1 + 10 cents: How many dimes?

11 dimes − 36 cents

$1.10 − 36 cents

19 dimes + 4 cents

$1.94 − 65 cents

String · D8

Partial Sums, Splitting, Standard Regrouping Algorithm

See D4 for details (page 66).

25 dimes + 5 pennies

24 dimes + 15 pennies

$2.50 − 9 cents

$2.50 − 19 cents

32 dimes + 6 pennies

$3.26 − 29 cents

String · D9

Using Landmark Numbers

This string of related problems encourages children to group using landmark numbers.

25 + 25 + 25 + 25

8 + 75 + 15 + 10 + 2

25 + 16 + 10

25 + 6 + 25 + 8

5 + 20 + 8 + 25

Behind the Numbers: How the String was Crafted

Since the string is designed to encourage grouping quarters, it begins with the reminder that four quarters make 100 cents. Most of the subsequent problems can be made easier if children group the coins to make quarters first. See D10 for additional support.

String · D10

Using Landmark Numbers

See D9 for details (page 68).

$$25 + 25 + 25 + 25$$
$$38 + 75 + 15 + 10 + 12$$
$$25 + 16 + 10 + 75$$
$$25 + 19 + 25 + 76$$
$$25 + 25 + 28 + 25$$